STILL LIFE

STILL LIFE

*SKETCHES FROM
A TUNBRIDGE WELLS
CHILDHOOD*

RICHARD COBB

faber and faber

TO
THE MEMORY OF MY MOTHER

This edition first published in 2008
by Faber and Faber Ltd
3 Queen Square, London WC1N 3AU

A CIP record for this book is available from the British Library

ISBN 978-0-571-24276-4

The town is never over-run with trippers,
nor are its streets ever defiled by the vulgar or
the inane. Its inhabitants are composed,
for the most part, of well-to-do people who
naturally create social atmosphere tinged by
culture and refinement . . .
On its outskirts are many houses of the kind
that attract those members of the aristocracy
desirous of change of scene
after the ceaseless social duties of the
London season. Thus it may be taken for
granted that when London is 'empty' in
the society sense, Tunbridge Wells is
at its liveliest and best.

From *Royal Tunbridge Wells:*
*The Official Guide, c.*1923

CONTENTS

The silhouette on page xvii
is of the author, aged 8½
by his mother Dora Cobb

A Bouquet for Tunbridge Wells
by J. C. Hall

Once, twice a year if work and funds permit it,
I board the quarter-to at Charing Cross
And diesel down on yet another visit
To my Good Place. Over the river, gross

Acres of brick wheel by, suburbs in flight.
Past Knockholt, the travelling sense anticipates
The first enormous tunnel – sudden night
(In the Steam Age a purgatory of smuts),

Then sudden daylight bursting on a world
Of hops and orchards. Soon, burrowing under Knole,
Another tunnel; then down the levelling Weald
To Tonbridge, printing works, a public school

I nearly went to. Ten minutes more, I'm there
At Tunbridge Wells' odd station, battened down
In a sort of hooded cutting as if to spare
The Victorian sensibilities of the town.

Though London-born, my life was anchored here
For fifteen years. A fabled place, yet boasting
Few of the Great. Victoria held it dear,
Thackeray did some growing-up, Pepys coached in,

Tennyson hurried out. This roll provides
Most of the famous. Maybe one day my friend
Keith Douglas, born here, will make the Guides.
Poets are legion. Time sorts us in the end.

But if not men, parks glorify this town.
Calverley, Nevill, Camden (rich images
Of lives we sigh for), a Common leading down
Into the busy streets by hilly stages,

True *rus in urbe*. And so much still complete,
So little spoiled, so little rearranged.
Pure nostalgia? Not quite. What's oversweet
Is harking back to something wholly changed.

Here forms survive, though all my kin are dead:
Our house, the boundary stream, the one-track line,
The bridge so low I start to duck my head,
St John's Wort in the hedge, and up the lane

That summer ground, so rhododendron-proud,
Where Woolley (they said), in one tremendous basting,
Lifted his longest six – over the crowd
Into a coal truck rumbling down to Hastings.

Yes, my Good Place. And though old-fashioned bores
May shake their heads and say the chap's not trusted,
Dear Tunbridge Wells, I sign this poem *Yours
Faithfully, Very Truly* – and not *Disgusted*.

PREFACE

From two recent visits I came back quite reassured. I had expected something much worse. At least the outer shell of continuity appeared to remain intact, whatever lay underneath. The Pantiles looked tatty and rather forlorn; several of the shops under the arcade were empty. Jupps had gone, there was an Indian restaurant, the big toy-shop and Dust's had disappeared. I even saw a violent drunk being led away, under the arcade, by two young policemen. I don't know what my mother would have made of that. The big house on the corner of Grove Hill and Claremont Road, in which Miss Vian, the sister of the Admiral, had lived in my mother's time, now proclaimed C N D messages from every groundfloor window and even from some upper-floor ones. The house next to it, once the home of Miss Meade-Waldo, one of my mother's favourite Bridge partners, now demonstrated, from *its* windows, a violent hostility to blood sports. The Hickmott empire had now extended right up the left side of Grove Hill, almost to the level of the entrance to Calverley Park, engulfing on its way the big house in which Dr Wood had lived and practised. There was something suitable about that: the Hickmott brothers, the younger of whom had been at school with me, were undertakers, so they had been in the same area of skills as Dr Wood; the Hickmotts worked from the terminus, the doctor had worked further up the line. One of the little stone archers and his crocodile guarding the entrance to Camden Park had gone, but his little companion – now all on his own and without his bow and arrow – was still there. Nevill Park seemed as affluent as ever, the houses as big as ever, and none of them had been taken over by insurance companies. Poona Road was still unmade, and still deep in yellow mud. Mrs Phillips' house overlooking the Happy Valley, in which the Basque children from Bilbao had been housed in 1938, and the German and Czech Jewish children, in 1939, had now become a hotel. The High Rocks looked frequented; but the little seat, facing the railway line, on which I had read about Carmen Silva, had been removed; and the footpath that had led from it through the woods under the overhanging rocks had been totally submerged in tall undergrowth. The Pulpit Tree was still in place, awaiting its preacher. A number of the smaller shops in the High Street had been replaced by estate agents, of which there appeared to be more than ever. There was a Spanish restaurant in Cumberland Walk. Lilac doors were beginning to appear down near Chapel Place. There were more antique-dealers than ever behind the Pantiles, an area now largely taken over by Pennink's, a family well known to my mother from the Bridge table. As with Hickmott's, I was glad of the evidence of a familiar name doing well.

The town looked somehow smaller, even Upper Grosvenor Road now seemed relatively close; but I found the Common more extensive than I remembered it, and the walk to the High Rocks and back by the Happy Valley quite tiring. A child's scale of measurement and awareness of orientation can also be revealed subsequently as wildly inaccurate. If you grow up in a town and live in it for many years, you probably do not think of it in relation to the points of the compass. As Grove Hill, Mount Sion and Little Mount Sion were steep arid went uphill, when I went up them, if I gave the matter a thought at all, I supposed I was going north, for north would seem to spell out extra effort, while going downhill, because it was easier, would suggest going south. Once at the age of twelve I had acquired a bicycle, I could situate Tunbridge Wells in relationship to the surrounding countryside, but I could never be certain whether I was getting the town itself the right way up. I might even mentally have got it upside-down. For over forty years, I had felt that going up Grove Hill was going north, I could *feel* it was going north. In fact, I had got Tunbridge Wells askew, as if it had toppled over on its side. It was only on my most recent visit, while comparing my memory and the mental picture I had retained of a town that I believed I knew inside-out, with the sober, unblinking realities of an Ordnance map of the Maidstone District (it should have been headed the Tunbridge Wells District), that I discovered, to my surprise and chagrin, that Grove Hill ran uphill in an *easterly* direction. It was almost as if I had been suddenly betrayed by an old and trusted friend, all at once revealed as having kept back from me for years a rather disreputable secret. But, even with the benefit of a knowledge come by so late, after so many years of error, I still have difficulty in putting the town back on its proper base. I still think of Grove Hill as climbing north. Perhaps it does not matter. But it seemed necessary to readjust all the orientations in the text that relate to the various approaches to the town, even if this seemed a breach of faith with my childhood. Tunbridge Wells is back the right way up.

No doubt memory often plays tricks of this kind. I was never a scout and never had any reason to learn to use a compass. It was enough to know that the morning sun came into my mother's dining-room and that the evening sun came in through the french windows of her drawing-room. I suspect that childhood memory often plays similar tricks. For myself, Frinton, where I was born, presented no problem; it was on the East Coast, the sea was to the east, Fourth Avenue could only extend inland, westwards. I found Le Havre and Aberystwyth similarly easy to come to terms with. But throughout my childhood, in my grandparents' lifetime, I had always mentally placed their part of Colchester, the Hythe, at the *southern* end of the town, because you went down hill to get there. Looking at a map of the Colchester area four or five years ago, I was amazed – and dismayed – to discover that the Hythe was at the *northern* tip of the town. This time I had indeed got the place upside-down. Yet Colchester has a river which, though it did not neatly divide the. town, should have made things easier. There is no river in Tunbridge Wells. For that matter, for quite a long time, I thought of the Porte d'Orléans as being at the northern exit from Paris. I had got Paris upside-down too.

What all this no doubt amounts to is that children, as well as long-term residents, do not give much attention to the points of the compass. I doubt whether Geoff Limbury-Buse could have charted his daily walk to and from the Tunbridge Wells and Counties Club. Why should he have done? He knew how to get there, and how to get back home. Before making the necessary readjustments to the compass, I found, in re-reading my text, that I even suggested, in the section entitled 'Figures in a Landscape', that, in his mind, he may have got Tunbridge Wells the wrong way up, or at least askew. I had not realised at that stage, that I had got Colchester the wrong way up, and Tunbridge Wells tilted on its side. There must have been town-plans in both places, but a child, or, indeed, any resident, would not think of looking at them. He would carry the town-plan in his head. As far as I am concerned, Grove Hill still climbs up north, guarded at its northern extremity by the surviving little stone archer. Childhood memory is more important, even if it gets things out of focus, than the unthinking, unimaginative accuracy of a compass or a map. I wrote this book with Tunbridge Wells tilting over at ninety degrees from north to east. As far as I am concerned, it will go on tilting over.

The town appeared to be largely unchanged but, of course, nearly everyone my mother and I had known had long been dead. Walking through the familiar streets, even though they no longer went in a familiar direction, and seeing the familiar houses, most of them unchanged, including the lovely Walmer Cottage at the foot of Mount Sion, was like walking through a place, the inhabitants of which had been struck down: here was the house in which my aunt Emily had died, here even was the

big balconied window of the room in which she had died. I
could have filled so many of the houses, big and small, with
their dead inhabitants, and I knew nothing of their living ones.
I even wondered if there were any people – perhaps one or two
of my contemporaries at Rose Hill – Pearmund, later a dentist,
Hickmott, if he could take his mind off the dead and remember
the living – in the town whom I would know or who would
know me. So I was very glad to see the lady at the counter in the
book section of Goulden & Curry, upstairs, standing in exactly
the same spot as she had occupied throughout my childhood;
Miss Woodhams is her name. She has worked in the shop for
fifty-nine years. I was not, after all, a complete stranger, not a
poor Joseph, back in his village, and shunned by all, as in
l'Histoire du Soldat. What is more, she even recognised me.

This is a book about growing up in a predominantly
middle-class community in the south-east in the twenties and
thirties. I have set out to rediscover the security and the
continuity of a society based on elaborate, if unstated,
hierarchies of class relations of considerable subtlety. It is a
study of a world of grown-ups as observed and partly
understood by a child between the ages of 4 and 13, and of an
increasing awareness of people and places during the years of
adolescence and youth. It concerns my relations with my
parents, with a retinue of aunts and uncles on my mother's side,
and with her extensive circle of middle-class friends; but I have
made room, too, for my own small group of local eccentrics. I
am attempting to illustrate a society both immensely self-
confident and largely immune from class conflict and social
tensions, and so one in which a rather frightened child could
feel immensely secure. And this sense of security would be
derived as much from *place* as from *people*, so I have set about
rediscovering the many fixed itineraries followed not only by
myself as a child, but also those of others encountered in the
course of these movements within the town and well beyond its
limits. Which people, where, and when: so, a chronicle also of

habit and routine, shopping and leisure: an attempt to place moving figures in a habitual landscape. Politics seem always to hover at several removes away in a society which seemed largely apolitical and from which the outside world was for a long time successfully excluded. Every person in his or her place, every object in its place, the whole town breathing regularly to a predictable time-table, everything as it should be, a place that was safe and cherished and remembered as such, but also a place of wonder and constant discovery.

As on a previous occasion, when I wrote about my grandparents, my uncle and my cousin Daisy, in my essay 'The House in the Hythe', included in *Places*, edited by Ronald Blythe, and published in 1981, my grateful thanks go to my sister, Mrs L.F. Papé, who has been infinitely patient in answering my queries and in rummaging in the enormous storehouse of her memories of Tunbridge Wells in the twenties, from a height seven years taller than my own, and thus commanding a much wider terrain. I am grateful to Mr and Mrs James B. Mennell Jr for having brought back to my vivid recollection the doleful figure of the Black Widow, as she haunted the macadam paths of the Common and for having supplied me with information about the Blue Mantles Cricket Club and for having recalled my mother's imperturbability during an Alert, engaged in planting seeds in her small front-garden. Mrs Mennell has also put me right on a number of points concerning the schools for girls in the town. I owe to my friend – and former pupil – Dr C.A. Bayly, Fellow of St Catharine's College, Cambridge, and at one time an inhabitant of Vale Royal (*behind* Mount Ephraim), his recollections of Skinners' School and of the tough country boys who walked there every day from villages as far distant as six or ten miles; he has also enriched me with his minute knowledge of the geology of the Common and of the fossils to be found near the Wellington Rocks. With Professor George Gillespie, Professor of German at University College, Cardiff, I share both a

Salopian experience – we were in the same awful House and suffered under the same awful Housemaster – and residence in the Royal Borough. Through him, I discovered, for the first time, the populous areas of the town behind the Old Town Hall, an area in which the pubs are particularly numerous and those who frequent them are particularly friendly. Through Professor Gillespie I was able to meet a number of his colleagues, at one time, like himself, teachers at Skinners'. He also added a new dimension to the existence of the Baltic Sawmills, in the person of his beautiful Latvian wife, Marika. My friend and former pupil, Lord Michael Pratt, has offered me glimpses of the Tunbridge Wells neighbourhood from an angle totally unfamiliar to me, adding his own memorable physical presence and his unforgettable voice to my awareness of the mute presence of his family in so many of the streets and Parks of the town: Camden Park, as it were, *fait personne*. Mr Paul Beale, now of Loughborough, and a member of a long-established family that has contributed in the past to much of the building of the residential areas of Tunbridge Wells, has been tireless in providing me with details from his own recollections – he followed me both to Miss Lake's and to Rose Hill – and those of his father, still a resident. He has also contributed to my knowledge of Goods Station Road. I had the good fortune of meeting Mrs Keith Douglas, the mother of the poet (a fellow Mertonian), at the party given in the Bodleian for the launching of the biography of her son, and she too was generous with her recollections as a long-term resident of one of the quiet roads behind the Pantiles.

I would like to take this opportunity of thanking most warmly Hugo Brunner, in his double capacity as editor and publisher. In the former, he has been ever-helpful with his suggestions and his encouragement; in the latter, he has brought to the necessarily close relations between author and publisher the extra quality of friendship. I have been most fortunate in both my editor and my publisher and each has been infinitely

patient in guiding an often untidy typescript towards pub-
lication.

Both my friend, and former pupil, Roger Butler, and my
wife, Margaret, have been very forbearing in listening to
chosen passages from this book of sketches. Mr Butler felt that I
had overpainted the Black Widow, so I took the hint, and toned
her down. My wife could also spot traces of over-writing in
certain extracts; and these, too, I have attempted to moderate.
The greatest danger in writing one's own childhood is a
tendency to archness. As attentive and critical listeners, Roger
Butler and my wife have been quick to detect possible traces of
this. I think that, as a result, they have all been dealt with.

Wolvercote, February, 1983

The opportunity provided by a second printing has enabled
me to correct some minor errors of fact and to include the poem
'A Bouquet for Tunbridge Wells' by my friend John Hall who
very kindly sent it to me after reading the book. He had written
it some months before.

November, 1983

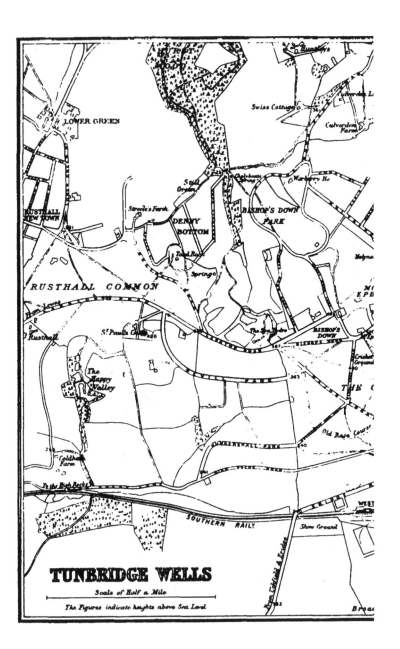

TUNBRIDGE WELLS

Scale of Half a Mile

The Figures indicate heights above Sea Level.

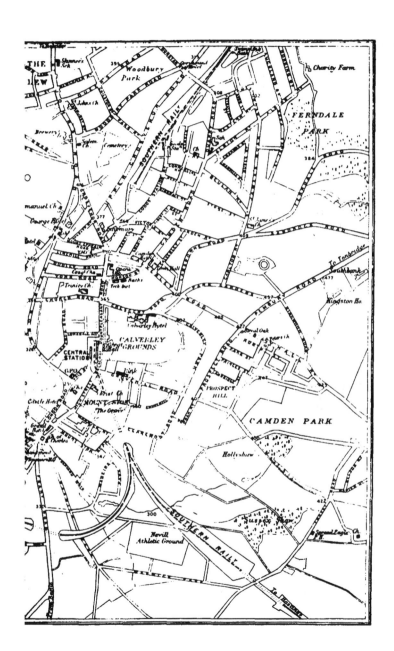

1 THE APPROACH

The approach to Tunbridge Wells by train, especially from the direction of London, is unexpectedly dramatic, and was even more so in the days of steam. The train starts to slow up while passing through High Brooms, an area to the north of the town certainly never visited by the inhabitants of the watering-place, and said to be inhabited, at least in my time, by 'very rough people'. Poor High Brooms! Even at the time of the General Strike, it had been completely dormant, the dailies, cooks and chars had turned up as usual, most of the buses had run, driven, like some of the trains, by the young bloods from Frant Road, Forest Road, Broadwater Down, Warwick Park, and the roads leading off Mount Ephraim. High Brooms was the object of silly jokes rather than one of foreboding and fear. But the *good* trains did not stop there, merely began to slow down. After skirting the Recreation Ground, still territory potentially dangerous, at least for middle-class children, the train entered a tube of mephistophelean darkness, shuddering in a mighty roar, to come to a halt at a platform just visible in a swirling fog of steam and soot. No sign of Tunbridge Wells; just a couple of steep wooden staircases (at one time displaying on each step the words 'Carter's Little Liver Pills', I don't know why, because the local waters were not for livers anyway) and, right at the top, after quite a climb, the barrier. The Central Station was in fact a suitable introduction to the many bizarreries that characterised the town, contributed to its uniqueness, and inspired in its more hardened residents a sort of amused affection. The station faced backwards, and was at two levels, so that passengers from London were greeted by the Traitor's Gate of the two smoky stairways, as much as to say: 'Just let

1

this teach you not to come here again', a point reinforced by the effort of having to drag every article of luggage up some twenty-five feet. Passengers *to* London, as if the Royal Borough were offering an award to visitors prepared to leave, in its haste to get rid of them and see them off the premises, would be confronted by the smiling, amiable side of the station, what in fact *looked* like the front: an elegant forecourt, a delicately tracered wooden canopy and a large, handsome ticket office, but which was, in reality, the *back*. Of course, there was no distinction between the Up platform and the Down one, both would be enveloped, as the line itself, in the swirling gloom of steam and soot – one could not see across to the other side, one could *hardly* see the train when it pulled up in the railway Hades – but, through the fog, one could hear the barking coughs of those heading for the seaside.

The Central Station was not only back-to-front, it had an immediate tunnel at *each* end, a freak of topography that contributed directly to the stygian gloom of both platforms. The train from London emerged from a tunnel the top of which was level with the lower slope of Mount Pleasant. There was a small footpath, reached by stone steps, that led just behind the coping of the top of the tunnel, a favourite vantage point for schoolboys as, listening to the onset, first of the full rumble, then the thunder of the approaching train, enclosed like a bullet in its tight barrel, they waited, with ever-renewed excitement, for the sudden puff, then the full and generous billow, like a yellow and white plume, of thick smoke and steam as it was driven forth just ahead of the front of the great green and gold engine. This was a spectacle denied one the other end where the tunnel cut through a hill at some distance from any path or road. But if one were waiting for the Up train well along the platform as it curled round, one would be rewarded once again, first with the rumble, as it rose to a crescendo of noise, then the little pre-puff, then the mighty multi-coloured billow, then with the sudden emergence of the beautiful green engine picked out with yellow piping, as it travelled still at speed. It was also easier to get a seat on one of the early-morning trains at this end, as it would necessitate walking the whole length of Charing Cross or Cannon Street on arrival. People who worked in the City – and, apparently, on the Stock Exchange, every second counted – would crowd into the front coaches, and sprint from Cannon Street, holding onto their bowlers, their umbrellas at right-angles.

The tunnel on the Hastings side went under the Grove. I used to enjoy the low rumble and the muffled shriek of the whistle when I was playing on the swings in this modest and rather unfashionable small park (the Royal Borough rather frowned on swings). The Grove was somewhat run-down; but it was the nearest playground to my successive homes in Claremont Road. I used to pretend that the very distinct rumble was the beginning of an earthquake, something that never came the way of Tunbridge Wells, though once when I was 6, there were hailstones as large as tennis balls. The storm was even reported in the Paris papers.

The Grove tunnel came out towards the bottom of the garden of Dr Ranking, half-way up Frant Road. I used to have tea at a lady's in the house opposite; if we were having tea in the garden, the saucers and plates would shake as the rumble all at once broke into a roar. I remember the lady for two reasons: her volcanic, hollow garden, and the pony-cart in which she would sometimes drive me to the High Rocks.

The result of this peculiar configuration was that it was impossible to see any of Tunbridge Wells from the train, at least on the London to Hastings line. After emerging at the bottom of the doctor's garden, the line ran through a deep cutting till it reached the open country. It seemed suitable that the town should have been preserved from the gaze of 'trippers', perhaps on a cheap-day-return to the sea. But the railways had not been placed underground because it was unsightly and ill-frequented, but because Tunbridge Wells was built on hills (seven, in all, including Mount Sion, Mount Ephraim, Mount Ararat, and the secular Mount Edgcumbe).

Also there *was* a railway-line – single track and very gingerly – that *did* go through the town. It connected the two stations – for, apart from the bizarre back-to-front Central with its operatic effects department, there was a much grander station, virtually a *terminus* (were it not for the single-track line), an impressive red-brick affair facing onto the Common, and called, according to choice, the West Station or the Brighton Station. This was the old LBSCR line that linked Tunbridge Wells with Crowborough, Uckfield, Lewes, and Brighton. The connecting line, after running through the Grove Tunnel, came out into the light at the bottom end of Madeira Park, crossing the private road leading to the Nevill Tennis Club over a low metal bridge. After skirting the wonders of Susie Willett's garden, it then ran beside a garden with a little stream and that was a blaze of daffodils in the spring, so close that it really seemed that the little train – generally only two carriages, pushed from behind by a busy, puffing tank engine, was actually *in* the garden. It was a most unusual, delightful and intruding line, for, far from revealing the backs of little brick houses, outside lavatories, washing lines and tiny squares of vegetation, it travelled slowly and very tentatively along an unwinding frieze of lush foliage, of tall pampas grass and bull-rushes, brilliant clumps of rhododendrons, wild roses, snap-dragons and red-hot pokers, herbaceous borders and smooth lawns with hammocks between the trees, as if all laid out uniquely for the passenger's delectation and to compensate him for the rude shock reserved for him by the Central Station. I suppose the ballast was not very even and that that was why the train had to go at such a snail's pace. But it seemed to be saying: 'Look, feast your eyes, this is the *real* Tunbridge Wells', it was such a private line, and, because it went so slowly, it did not make much noise. I have talked to people whose gardens ended onto this line, and they have told me that they

4

regarded the little train, not as a cheeky intruder, but as a discreet and welcomed friend. (Each time, long after my childhood, I came over from Paris, via Newhaven, and changing at Lewes, I would offer myself the delight of thus entering Tunbridge Wells along a fringe of well-kept and luxuriant gardens, before rattling through the choking Ghost Train effect of the Grove tunnel.)

Nor was this the only delight awaiting the traveller to or from Brighton. The approach to Tunbridge Wells West, after Groombridge station, would take one rattling merrily below the High Rocks, past an oast-house, then more rocks capped with dark trees with prehensile roots – an illustration from a Gothic novel – by the side of a pretty road, a glimpse of the Common and finally the agricultural show ground and the Baltic Sawmills (I liked the Baltic bit, it seemed to lend Tunbridge Wells the pale glamour of the Northern Lights, though this was nonsense, for the firm was run by the father of a Rose Hill school friend of mine; but the boy *did* have very pale blue eyes and the wood *did* come from Riga). It was a gentle approach, suitably orchestrated by the merry rattle of the little train as, going quite fast, it echoed against the steep sides of the High Rocks. No High Brooms, though, this entry, but just a glimpse of the big houses – some of them I knew only too well – belonging to dentists, at the bottom end of Hungershall Park. In winter, when one could see further and pick out objects more clearly, I could even see my Pulpit Tree, a stopping-place on one of my favourite walks, when I would run ahead of my parents, so as to greet them from the pulpit, two branches that came together high up the bank, so that I was raised up well above the footpath: a pulpit or a lectern, it did not matter, I was addressing the multitude, their faces upturned, as they listened in wrapt attention.

An approach from the north by road would be less dramatic than the sudden plunge into the Central Station (which did have *one* advantage: if one were leaving for boarding-school, the swaying smoke and steam would at once obscure the last view of waving parents, making the sudden break easier to bear, and preventing shaming tears – though these would not be seen in the tunnel); but it had little to recommend it if one were coming from London, as it would take one through the dreary, sprawling ribbon of houses, most of them both classless and pretentious, monuments to the jerry-building of the twenties, a spreading, anonymous, long-drawn-out suburb linking South-borough and its dusty common with Tunbridge Wells, and lined by the round Christian Science church that looked like an ice-rink, and the borstal-like buildings, in livid brick of Skinners' School. It brought one in the wrong way, past motor-showrooms (in the thirties, ugly things like that were, properly, hidden away in the least desirable quarters of the town, and the presence of which marked such quarters out as being third-rate and tawdry) down steeply to the level of the Five Ways, with its big public convenience, then the Opera House and the offices of the Maidstone & District bus company, to the War Memorial, as it gazed bewilderingly at the early mock-Gothic arch leading to Holy Trinity church. There *had* to be a War Memorial; but it had been sited beyond the top of Mount Pleasant, which marked the frontier between the predominantly middle-class area extending from the Pump Room at the far end of the Pantiles to the Cadena near the top of Mount Pleasant, and the ill-defined population of Monson Road and Calverley Road. The War Memorial was firmly placed on the wrong side of the frontier.

The greatest surprise would be provided by the approach from the south, along the beautiful route of the Southdown buses – their light green carrying something of the freshness of downland and heath with them – that went all the way from Brighton to faraway Gravesend (though it would be hard to imagine anyone doing the whole diagonal trip from the one terminus to the other). This was also the rich man's likeliest route, bringing the golfers back from the prestigious Crow-

6

borough links and those who rode with the Eridge Hunt. After Eridge, the road climbed up steeply through the enormous trees of the Park, past many Gothic gates marked 'A' (for Abergavenny, Marquis of – the Nevill family), and through the young silver-birch and fledgling firs growing on the sandy soil of Broadwater Forest. At the top of the rise, there was a small crossroads, from which the main road curled steeply downwards towards the town. All one could see from the crossroads, lined up in the late-afternoon sun, were the great white, yellow and pink blocks of the hotels on Mount Ephraim, as if Tunbridge Wells consisted only of that illustrious and luminous high ridge, floating in the sky. Even after years, it came to me with the same sudden sense of surprise and pleasure, the proud flag of a town built for leisure, for quiet and orderly enjoyment, for rather dowdy comfort and old-fashioned luxury, and inhabited above all by those long past their prime. It was, of course, quite out of scale with the poky little houses in which we lived during most of my childhood. But one felt that the whole town and every one of its inhabitants benefited in some way from the proximity of Mount Ephraim, which seemed somehow to pull everything and everyone up to its own proud and very superior level. It would have been nice to have lived on Mount Ephraim – for long one of the will-o'-the-wisps flittingly followed by my parents: first, an early-Victorian white house with wrought-iron green balconies, its walls covered in wisteria, then an elegant little jewel-box of a Regency house with long windows. The best dentists (but not the best doctors, less ostentatious) and elderly retired female courtiers – ladies-in-waiting to Queen Alexandra, even to Queen Victoria – did live there. The only snag would be that, if one lived on Mount Ephraim, one could not look at it. And it was best seen, most appreciated, from afar. Once past the crossroads, as one came rushing down the steep hill, Mount Ephraim would disappear, as though swallowed up. But one would still come in along the edge of the Common and by the

Brighton Lake, in reality a tiny pond so overgrown with reeds and vegetation that the water was scarcely visible, and then along the back of the Pantiles, which, because it was the back, and so not meant to be shown off, looked rather miserable, as if one had just stumbled on a sordid secret or caught someone in the midst of a furtive and tawdry action, who believed that he were unobserved. The back of the Pantiles was like backstage, was not supposed to be seen, much less walked up and down on; the shops did not face that way, and the only display window on that side was a motor-car saleroom, a line of business suitably cast out from the closed promenade, the cars facing bleakly up Major York's Road.

The town with the back-to-front station and so many parks, crescents and circuses had many problems of this kind. The proud crescents did not look so proud from the back, curving the wrong way, their backs lined with a jagged grill of black iron fire-escapes and dust-bins. Even the elegant Calverley Park, sweeping in a very gentle curve and overlooking a couple of magnificent cedars and the green bowl of grass that fell with quiet ease towards the tennis-courts and the municipal gardens, even Calverley Park, the houses of which, according to their position in the curve, had a view of a blue and misty Crowborough Beacon, of Mount Ephraim, had a back which faced east, and grimly, onto the wrong end of Pembury Road. I suppose these were the entrances used by the servants, still numerous in these big houses, shut away from the rest of the town by a monumental arch at the far end, and protected by two more lodges and gates at the other two entrances. The servants, if they lived in Hawkenbury, would not have far to come. I was very early on fascinated by the *back* of Calverley Park – my parents, my sister and I regularly used the footpath that cut in a straight line across the front – it seemed such a give-away. It was a (slightly) guilty secret that I shared with myself. It would have been hard to explain why I had sought it out in the first place, and why I so much enjoyed going past the long, inverted curve of tiny windows and unassuming doors, most of them up iron staircases.

But much the best approach to the town was on foot. For one thing, this would offer an extraordinarily wide variety of vegetation, so that one could change continents and latitudes in the course of quite a short walk. If one approached the centre of the town from any part of Mount Ephraim, Nevill Park, or the High Rocks, one would find oneself (that is, if one 6 or 10, and still quite small) walking under the bright green umbrella, penetrated here and there by shafts of brilliant sunshine, of the tropical rain-forest – grown-ups might have called them ferns, but they did grow four or five feet high, and a small boy could look up to their jagged leaves as they swayed gently in the tropical wind. The Congo, Java, Borneo, the Gran Chaco lay, for those in the know, within a few hundred yards of the Pantiles and of King Charles the Martyr. Even the most banal walk – cutting through from the level of the footpath above the Brighton Lake, crossing at right angles two tarmac paths – could bring one crashing through thick, almost impenetrable jungle which would open all at once on sudden clearings, hidden by the thick lines of tropical vegetation. The jungle clustered, in vivid greens, on the lower slopes, thickening as one approached the town. Did my mother's tweed and jaeger-clad and sensibly-shoed friends who regularly took their elevenses at the Orange Tea Rooms in the Pantiles realise that they were on the very edge of the jungle, its dark green shadows echoing to the hideous cries of exotic beasts? They did not show any signs of awareness that they were sitting at the extreme tip of a very thin crust of civilisation.

But, before striding down into the green tanglia of the jungle rain-forest, the walker from the heights of Mount Ephraim had to struggle, in heavy boots and the necessary tackle, over mountainous terrain: the Wellington Rocks, the even more treacherous range, with exotic plants growing in the deep, black interspaces between the strangely-shaped dark grey and

9

greenish rocks that provided an almost insurmountable barrier for one attempting to approach the town – and no approach on foot could be allowed to be easy – from Boyne Park and the Earl's Court Hotel: a wild, northern, tulgy scene, rock-strewn, terrible chasms, grotesque trees showing all their roots. And, beyond, the grove of trees planted for Queen Victoria's Jubilee and a thatch-topped shelter with old ladies sitting in it reading books marked with the green and white shield of Boots Circulating Library.

A walker approaching from the north-west, the direction of Speldhurst, would have to cross three distinct climatic zones: the dark forest (containing one of the five local resident hermits); the dank savannahs in which huge, sweating Victorian houses, their walls almost black with zebra lines of dark green damp, suppurated among damp firs, dark yews and tearful monkey-puzzle trees. This was an opaque zone, smelling of mould and decay, the houses showing no sign of life, save for curtains in dirty materials and a few damp-looking black cats; a place deeply romantic for the young walker, all the more surprised, therefore, suddenly to leave the dark, dripping trough behind him to emerge into the brilliant light in the 'South of France' – for so it was called locally by people who had never been to the real one – a row of comfortable wooden seats set against a crenellated pseudo-Gothic wall topped by a couple of false ruins in high-Victorian medieval style, that offered protection from the north. The South of France looked in the direction of the Spa Hotel, over a tulgy piece of overgrown ferns and assorted weeds and was favoured by many seated muffled figures basking in the timid sunshine. It was hard to get a seat there; it was a sort of outside Wellington Hotel when the old ladies and the old gentlemen came out from behind plated glass. My mother, who always had lunch at midday and who could walk quite fast well on into her seventies, could generally beat the Wellingtonians to it, cutting down through Little Mount Sion, then right across the Common, past the Wellington

Rocks, to reach the South of France by one, while the regulars were still at lunch. It was one of her favourite seats, but as she reached her late-seventies, she had to give up her trips to the local Riviera, it was too hard going.

All these, the best approaches, were from the south-west and the east. The approach from the west was unrelievedly urban and firmly set in south-east England at its worst, and mostly, in the less distinguished, more cheap-jack twenties, though there were one or two dark recesses on the way. They were dramatic, in a restrained and pretty sort of way, for, having struggled through the dark forest, the dank savannah, or negotiated the rock-infested escarpments, clung on to overhanging roots, and used a breast-stroke motion with one's fore-arms to brush aside the tall ferns overlooking the hermits' caves, one was offered all at once three-quarters of Tunbridge Wells on a plate, spread out in spires, domes, towers, clumps of trees and circuses, the roof of the Eye and Ear Hospital, the whole topped by the thin line of pine trees marking out Forest Road, from Thackeray's House and Holy Trinity, to King Charles, the Pump Room, and the needle spire of Broadwater church pricking through the monkey-puzzle trees, with Gibraltar House and St Helena Cottage built into its over-shadowing rock in the left foreground, as if inviting an aquatint: *A View from Mount Ephraim*. It was in fact just the sort of thing that went onto the covers of wooden boxes in dark and light brown check patterns known as Tunbridge Ware.

The approaches from the north were fewer and were known only to the servant population of Hawkenbury, to the small farmers who supplied the Calverley Road market, and to the more adventurous walkers (the cemetery and the golf club, both on the northern approaches, would have drawn only motorised travellers, living or deceased, walkers tending to give the Isolation Hospital and the sewage farm a wide berth). Yet these less numerous approaches offered quite a wide range of climatic zones: savannahs, yes, of course, as dank and as dripping as those of the south; also a thin line of pines, spread out like the hairs on the back of a wild pig, outlined against the sky; areas of gorse and broom; even river country, for a tiny, brownish stream that provided the ink-tasting waters and the Chalybeate Spring in the Pantiles ran between steep banks thick with buttercups, and under a pretty little bridge. Pony-carts came this way in the late twenties, their hatted female drivers in search of bluebells and primroses in the thin woodlands on the edge of the Bayham Estate. This road ran on one side topped by a very steep bank covered in wild strawberries and violets, blackberry thickets (near the sewage farm), even a well, and, near it – at the bottom of a very steep hill – small farms, one flanked by two oast-houses, allotments, a cinder path leading to the High Woods, even a ruin, that of the Culpeper mansion, standing in a farmyard and gauntly visible from the cinder path. As one approached the town, one cut through a small recreation ground, some modern almshouses and the vaguely disreputable Hawkenbury (the children were quite alarming) and then through an unmade road past an ugly rash of Government pre-fabs and a small, scruffy field in which there was, in all seasons, a small tent, the home of one of the local hermits, and the one most often seen in the north end of the town, wearing an old blazer, yellowing cricket ducks, and old gym shoes, with longish yellow hair and a scraggy yellowish beard, talking to himself rather emphatically, in a good accent, and hawking matches, boot polish and scrubbing brushes from door to door in Calverley Park and Claremont Road. It was perhaps an area more *English* – small copses, masses of squelchy yellow mud to match the iron-water of the stream, footpaths through fields and young woods, a cross-roads in the woods with a tiny green and three thatched cottages, as if the whole thing had strayed from an illustration in a *Country Life* calendar. Few people came this way, for there not anywhere to come from, the little, narrow roads between steep banks and tall hedges, did not lead to or from any village, and one encountered very little traffic, so that it was generally quite safe to walk in the middle of the road.

It was enclosed and rather secret country, with no horizons; one could nowhere see very far, so it was very difficult to relate it to anywhere else and to fit it into the discipline of the points of the compass. All one knew for certain was that Tunbridge Wells was behind or ahead and that it could be approached either by the footpath that led from the top of Forest Road, through fields with sheep and a scattering of ugly new houses, to the middle of Claremont Road, or by the unmade road, near the tented hermit's encampment – the more rewarding route, for, as one turned the corner, and up a steep hill between rhododendron bushes, one reached at the top what was certainly the most bizarre of the entries to the town: a sort of Victorian *octroi*, the tiny lodge at the entry to Camden Park (everything was Camden to the north, just as everything was Nevill to the east), its minuscule garden decorated by two little stone men, covered in shells and holding tiny metal bows and arrows, seated on two stone crocodiles, likewise encrusted with shells. They seemed to be the guardians at the gates, holding the frontier between the gloomy Camden Park and the staid yellow stucco heights of Grove Hill, the beginning of Tunbridge Wells proper. As long as they remained in place, the town could come to no harm. For a cunning invader might attempt to step in through this little-known and little used approach.

There was no approach to the town from the air, no airfield anywhere near, and very little level ground in the town of seven hills, many rocks and promontories, deep, steaming sloughs, and thick undergrowth. I suppose a plane could have landed on the Nevill Cricket Ground, but what a fuss there would have been! A plane could have landed, at a pinch, and rather bumpily, on the Linden Park Cricket Ground, at the top of the Common; there would have been less fuss, but the plane would have been in danger of crashing into the Wellington Rocks, just as that mysterious machine bearing R A F markings and made largely of canvas, cotton and a very light wooden frame, had apparently crashed among the High Rocks in 1918 or 1919, and had then lain in its various severed bits, its engine still smelling strongly of petrol, throughout the twenties, when its scattered presence was used by me as a strong argument in favour of the High Rocks walk.

I have been told by those who have flown over the town – and this must have been the experience of many young Luftwaffe pilots, few of whom can ever have seen the place from the ground – that, owing to the huge extent of the Common and the various parks, and the sports grounds, it was so heavily treed as to be virtually invisible from the air, at least in summer. The town did indeed receive a number of German bombs, but these were rather insulting ones; they do not appear to have been *meant* for Tunbridge Wells, but were probably left-overs from London raids, that were discarded, in this casual and impertinent manner, before the pilots headed back across the Channel. Most of these bombs destroyed large middle-class houses, and their inhabitants, including the resident servants, in such respectable areas as Lansdowne Road. I recall one large yellow house, its cornices and window-ledges picked out in chocolate – a favourite combination in the area beyond Calverley Park – that had been cut right down one side, revealing the flowered wall-papers of drawing-room, dining-room and hall, all familiar to me because the house belonged to one of my mother's Bridge friends, and I had often been there for tea, between two rubbers, as a schoolboy. What seemed most horrifying was this breach of privacy, the indecent exposure of what had never been supposed to have been seen: the inside of bedrooms, the patterns of their wall-paper. Though I had been to the house many times, I had, of course, never been beyond the ground-floor. It was an outrage. Tunbridge Wells Bridge players did not get killed in war, nor their large houses get thrown open to the public stare. It made me realise how close war could be to revolution. Lansdowne Road . . . then, it would have been hard *not* to have hit a middle-class target in a town such as the Royal Borough. One of the buildings hit, it is true, was a *factory*; but it was a very small factory, and manufactured Romary's Water Biscuits, and these were very middle-class biscuits, indeed the cream of middle-class biscuits, bringing national fame to the town from the reign of William IV. German pilots, either alive and by parachute, or dead, in the wreckage of their machines – or lynched by the Cockney hop-pickers, so it was rumoured of one in 1940, though it was probably just one of many rumours that circulated during that dreadful summer – did land among the hopfields north of the town, or on Crowborough golf course and on Ashdown Forest. A pair of long boots came through the roof of a conservatory in a rectory garden near Brenchley – I was informed of this gruesome detail by my mother's daily, who was generally reliable in such items of local news – but none came down in Tunbridge Wells itself.

So, in a period when a great many people took walks – for enjoyment, for exercise, or simply to get from one place to another (a number of boys at Skinners' School walked in every day from villages as far away as Mayfield, Frant, Groombridge, and Langton), there were a great many possible approaches to the town, though none as dramatic as the experience of arrival at the Central Station. But perhaps I have been defining approaches within too narrow a radius and in a sense too strictly physical. Could not the approach be put back to what was so often the starting-point, the far-right-hand platform of Charing Cross? Could not the returning emissaries of the Wells be identified in the groups of sensibly-dressed ladies in their forties, fifties and sixties, hatted and gloved, and talking in confident and clear tones – they did not seem to be concerned about being overheard – about how they had spent the morning and the afternoon 'in town'? Harrods, Swan & Edgar (that sensible shop that must have clothed at least a quarter of the population of the town), Peter Robinson, lunch at one of the big stores, a walk in St James's Park, tea at a hotel in Piccadilly, then to Charing Cross, no rush at all, London is such a tiring place. . . . And so it would go on, easily audible and carefully enunciated, and with a great deal of underlining – simply *frightful*, I just didn't know where to look, what a terrible *faux-pas* (fo-pah), a fright of a frock, Dr Grace's daughter, the *younger* one, very hard on the *parents*, poor things. I said why did you lead with *hearts* (the very voice of the Royal Borough, and that of my mother, reproachful, at her breakfast-table post-mortems on my father's previous day's performance with Culbertson), she's grown into quite a little *hussy*, a face like *Jezebel* – through Chislehurst, Orpington, Sevenoaks, Hildenborough, and Tonbridge. One knew, both from the clothes, the shoes, the packages bearing the names of big shops, and the utterly confident tones, that none would get out at any of these places, and it came as no surprise that, at the level of the Recreation Ground, each would start gathering her packages together, look in her purse for the ticket, adjust her hat, using an improbably sunny picture of Bexhill – Southern Railway water-colour – as a mirror, before standing expectantly in the corridor during the roaring passage through the tunnel. Much banging of doors, almost the whole train getting off. Where else would they go? Did they *look* like travellers to Hastings? There was something wonderful about the unspoken assumption of *everyone's* (*everyone*, heavily underlined, had recurred frequently: *everyone* does it now, *everyone*, absolutely *everyone*, during the trip, even while under the North Downs, running neck-&-neck with *nobody*: of course, she was a *nobody* before she married, *nobody* would, well *would* they?) destination. A lot of them had no doubt gone up on the same train at 9 or 10 in the morning, after the business rush. And, all the way, both ways, they carried Tunbridge Wells with them; it hung in the smoky (South London) air between them, it was in their clothes

and their tasteful, discreet, unostentatious jewellery, it was in
the muted colours of their scarves, their blouses, their little silk
handkerchieves, in the library book that they carried but which
they did not read, it was in their washed-out, blue eyes and in
the clearly-marked deltas of mauve veins, extensive estuaries –
the Brahmaputra at least – that gave to their weather-beaten red
faces a hint of intelligence and even kindness, it was in their
thick stockings, it was above all in their emphatic and utterly
confident speech – a communication between equals (the pitch
would have been lowered when addressed, by surname, to
servants: 'Hale, would you please see. to . . .'), a mutual
recognition of the right sort of accent, the emission and
reception of a verbal semaphore in a recognised code that would
exclude others. Never a glance out of the window, not even a
look at the rigging, derricks, funnels and masts of the ships
clustering beyond Tower Bridge, nor for the tiny Gustave Doré
brick houses, in curling rows, huddling deep below the steep
railway embankment, each with billowing lines of washing. A
complete failure even to notice that other sudden wealth of
colour amidst the prevailing blackish brick and slate grey: the
pretty semaphore of flags and signals, hanging from the triple
masts of a flag manufacturer and flapping happily right beside
the line, on the *down* side, just before New Cross. Not even a
sidelong look at poor, dowdy Chislehurst, a one-time would-be
Tunbridge Wells, but now sinking into mere suburbia, almost a
standing joke for not having made it. Never a pause to look at
the beautiful gentle fold of the southern slope of the North
Downs, golden in the afternoon sun, revealed all at once as the
train emerged from a long tunnel. Why look at Sevenoaks? No
eyes for the hop-fields, the hops almost fully grown, before
Hildenborough – what would they know about hops, about
beer, about pubs? They might have heard vague reports about
hop-*pickers* from South London, how rough and dirty their
children were, and ill-spoken too, a preview of similar litanies
on the subject of the evacuees at the beginning of the War. No

17

eyes for the two narrow curling channels of the Medway, a
democratic river with rowing boats to be hired by the hour,
opposite the Castle (my annual birthday treat on 20 May, a treat
indeed when one lived in waterless Tunbridge Wells) as it ran
through the big meadow at the approach to Tonbridge. No
recognition of the big black letters spelling out 'Woolley Cricket
Balls', on a wall a little before Tonbridge Station. Woolley had
been a Player, not a Gentleman, and now he was in trade (and
lived in Tonbridge, which was rumoured to contain people who
were 'Labour'). No taking in of the view east, towards a deep
gap in the contours of the land, indicating the invisible and
widening Medway towards Wateringbury, with two oast-
houses and a clapboard cottage in the foreground, seen from the
brick viaduct between Tonbridge and High Brooms, nor, from
the other window, of the dark form of Bidborough Ridge; and,
of course, no one (*nobody*) would even give High Brooms a
distasteful glance, not a *place*, just a sordid word. It was not
their eyes, but their ears, that warned them of the approach of
their common destination, the increased volume of sound as the
train started braking, before entering the final tunnel. And
what did the *train* say? Swan & Edgar, Dickins & Jones, Peter
Robinson, very fast as it ran downhill after coming out of the
tunnel through the Downs, slower and slower, lower and lower,
almost a whisper, as it headed towards the curved platform of
the Central.

Or take the 5.50 from Cannon Street, a different regiment,
and a different, but equally uniform sex, but still in the
mutually recognisable uniforms (Tunbridge Wells was a place
where clothes called to clothes, cutting out words and
greetings) of Boyne Park, Molyneux Park, Frant Road,
Warwick Park (but not Broadwater Down, which would go by
road self-driven or chauffeur-driven): dark blue three-piece
pin-stripe, Van Heusen (semi-stiff) white collars on (Viyella)
shirts in blue-and-white or red-and-white stripes (some of the
stripes a bit on the wide side, not *quite* the thing, maybe *not*

Molyneux Park), protruding cuffs held by (discreet) gold or silver cuff-links, polka-dot ties, white on blue or white on red silk handkerchieves to match, or silk Old School ties (Lancing, Tonbridge, Canford, Haileybury, Eastbourne, Radley, Sutton Valence, Merchant Taylors, Bradfield), or those of the Blue Mantles Cricket Club, plus the regulation accompanying kit: bowler, rolled-up umbrella, battered and smudged *Daily Telegraph*, despatch case in pale pigskin (but not *too* pale), bought at the leather shop, Pullan's, on the London Road – sandy moustache optional, but not obligatory, voices loud, fruity, throaty, wheezy, laugh penetrating, forced, horsey, neighing, offensive, jokes unsubtle, *risqué*, predictable; stance: standing at the bar, facing mirror-image; faces, pink to scarlet, touches of mauve, eyes pale-blue and watery, eyebrows sandy and curling in little horns, at the ends; activity: drinking double-gin-and-its, large whisky-and-sodas. The 5.50 was *the* liquid train – 6 to 7 doubles between Cannon Street and the Wells – and so one that sought out the hard core of the 25 to 55 alcoholic age-group. The 6 to 7 doubles were all known by name, they were always the same, monopolising the bar, bagging the best places minutes before the train's departure. Later, they could be seen staggering up the steep paths of the Common, past Gibraltar House, puffing and blowing, their cheeks blown out or sagging mauvely, strung along the way, like an army in defeat, their moustaches damp, their faces red and sweaty, while others lay back, like washed-up whales, on the wooden seats orientated towards a hypothetical evening sun, and designed, in fact, for elderly ladies and gentlemen, the latter who had either long given up the daily shuttle of *up* and then *down*, or, like my cousins (who were said to be delicate), had never worked at all. There they sat, scattered at different levels – some had *almost* reached the top – like identical broken dolls, their bowlers on the seat beside them, revealing their silk interiors, the owner's initials in gold, and the name 'Home Bros.', or pushed over their eyes, as if they had been bookies,

19

and not young or middle-aged men who worked in the City. Observers on the top would know that the 5.50 was in, had been for some time, must be about 7.15, for these were the rearguard, the walking wounded; the alert, those who had slept the whole way from Cannon Street to High Brooms, waking up by habit just at the level of the Recreation Ground, had been seen at 6.50 on the dot striding up the tarmac paths, swinging their umbrellas at right angles, or heading through the High Street in the direction of Frant Road. The army was in, could be accounted for, there were no casualties, only one or two who had fallen out of the stationary train and who had been helped up, before it continued on what was now its futile journey, carrying a few lonely figures, not members of the regiment, on to Frant, Wadhurst and all those other places – a spoken or broadcast litany which one knew by heart but to which no one paid the slightest attention, unknown uncared-for territory, *outre*-Tunbridge Wells, a *beyond* that defied the perhaps sluggish imagination of those who shuttled *up*, then *down*, sober *up*, less so, or fast asleep, *down*.

Or take the 10.50 p.m. from Charing Cross during the Christmas holidays. Boys, in grey flannel suits or shorts, Viyella shirts in light and dark brown, or green and brown cross-hatches, ties in vertical stripes in two colours, their shorts or trousers held up with black and red belts attached by a silver buckle representing a serpent turning in on itself and biting its own tail: legs outstretched, or, if not reprimanded, on the opposite seat, tired but satisfied. Girls, well much the same: grey flannel, Viyella, worsted stockings, felt hats, but sitting up, more wide awake and chattering in clear, confident tones, in their no-nonsense voices, to their sensibly-clothed parent, or parents. Oh Mummy, wasn't it a *scream*! I loved the bit when he hid behind the curtain, it was a *hoot*; and when his wig fell off, I could have *died*. They've been taken to a *show* (we know *what* show) in *town*, it is the holidays anyway, it'll be almost midnight by the time they *get in* (meaning, of course,

The Approach

Tunbridge Wells, where else, silly fool?), there are generally plenty of taxis outside the taxi-office on Mount Pleasant. A desultory conversation through the night, or parents nodding, then suddenly pulling themselves out of encroaching sleep. Which tunnel was *that*? Are we there already? Best to count them. The one that matters is the *fourth*.

Or take the 12.15 from Charing Cross, the last train home. Two fair-haired teen-age girls with china blue eyes expressing a unique combination of boredom, contempt, vacuity, and self-assurance, and, at the moment, slightly fixed, silk party dresses and smart white shoes, long white gloves covering the fore-arm, little bags in coloured silk, with mother-of-pearl clasps, and bobbles hanging from them, fur-coated – they must be sisters – accompanied by their mother – the girls, excited and flushed and rather drunk, their eyes too fixed to give the normal message of disdain, their armoured defences not fully manned, one of them attempting to adjust her mouth, which appears to have gone askew, twisting sideways, and giving her an expression both startled and comical: dab, dab, dab, she only makes it worse. You do look a sight, Daphne, says the mother. Still, you seem to have enjoyed yourself. What about you, Peggy? I do hope James is there to meet us with the car, it is *such* a job to get a taxi. That was *such* a nice young man, and very good-looking too. He told me he was going to the Varsity, and was looking forward to it. A bit *brainy*, I expect, but he doesn't *look* it, and he was very considerate and attentive and he kept on getting me a glass. I must say I enjoyed myself. It's a bit of an effort getting up to one of these things, but it's so much worth it for you girls. And you'll have so much to tell your friends. I *bet* they've never been to anything like that. One does sometimes feel a bit cut *off*; but there are so many compensations, and you know where you are and what to expect. And it's excellent for shopping – not quite like *town*, perhaps, but you can't expect everything, and there really is always an awful lot going on, and it's very healthy, not down by

21

the High Street, of course, but no one lives there anyhow; one of the doctors said . . . Tonbridge, already. Don't forget your bag. I *do* hope James has remembered. I did remind him, he is pretty reliable, *such* a find. Be careful of the step when you get out, we're in the middle of the train, I'd take your shoes off, if I were you, hold them in your hand, I'm simply terrified of that gap. I hope that nice man is on the barrier, he's so polite, always has a word. Makes one glad to be back. Yes, *there* he is. Be careful not to trip up coming up the stairs, I'd lift up your shawl if I were you. And there's James. Well, here we are. Whatever you may say, it's nice to be back.

2 LOCATIONS

Getting there is part of *being* there, and the town exists on several dimensions at once. I used to carry bits of it away with me to Paris; the Toad Rock would suddenly turn up uninvited in the rue de Tournon. The Toad Rock at Rusthall was a symbol, for, at the end of one summer holiday, I carved my name on it with my pen-knife (it may still be there) in an effort to prolong the holiday and my Tunbridge Wells presence by leaving something of me behind there: a pathetic attempt to cheat the inevitable return to school and the advent of term similar to my habit of stuffing my pockets with the torn-off last few days of August and early-September, in the same way as I'd keep used Maidstone & District or Southdown bus tickets, or cinema tickets, from the Great Hall and the Kosmos. Looking at the paper rectangle Monday 24 August, in my study, in the faraway north (Shrewsbury: I had travelled farther, in England at least, than any member of my family, except my mother who had spent a brief spell teaching at a girls' school in New Brighton), I would try and reconstruct exactly how I had spent that day, back in a recent, golden past, so that I could offer myself a regular ration of the Royal Borough, in a place in which, initially, I did not want to be, where I felt a trembling stranger, and where I could not be *alone*. The enormous luxury, the unique wealth that Tunbridge Wells could offer me is that I *còuld* be alone, anywhere, in all sorts of places, even among other people, so intense was my awareness of each familiar location and its association with some particular events, some personal experience, even some *thought*. An exact spot on the Old Race Course is marked by my feeling of excitement, on a summer day when I was 8 or 9, while I was kicking a ball into the tall ferns, at the prospect that, the following day, I was going on a journey to the far North: in fact, to Northampton, to stay with a clergyman friend of my father's. I can exactly locate my ninth birthday by the fact that I spent part of the morning walking along the top of a lowish wall that divided Cumberland Gardens from the big doctor's house up a drive off Mount Sion. A five-barred gate to a field half-way down the steep hill leading from the Happy Valley to the High Rocks is *the* gate, not just any *other* five-barred gate, because it was the one I used to walk along the top of, holding out my arms to keep my balance, as I swerved from side to side, in the tolerant, and not very impressed presence of my mother; still, I generally managed to make it from one end to the other. But why *that* gate? I have no idea, it must have had something to do with my mania for routine, for continuity, as a protection against the terrible things that might come from *outside*: outside Tunbridge Wells. At the bottom of the hill, the High Rocks can never escape the peculiar smell of the broken aeroplane – a combination of the acrid odour of hemp and that of petrol. A seat below a rock that faced onto the little railway line, further towards the town, is inseparable from Carmen Silva, the poetess Queen of Roumania, about whom I was reading (I always took books on walks) one afternoon I stopped there; I thought what beautiful names she had. A winter's evening, walking up Grove Hill with my friend Bobby Atholl, is preserved in a still: the pale gas lamps sighing gently, giving a soft light to the pink-and-blue brick pavement, the double archway, much more impressive at night, almost Roman, leading to Birdcage Walk, a whitish and familiar presence, the last landmark on the tiring journey up hill and home; we had been having a deeply serious conversation about Life, as between two experienced ten-year-olds. 'I suppose the happiest time of one's life was when one was a baby', said one of us ponderously, a remark both pretentious and presumably inaccurate, though deeply felt by both of us on that silent gas-lit evening – and, there it is, still hanging about the double-arch of Birdcage Walk.

A certain part of the Common, the first bit of level ground off the path leading diagonally from opposite the red General Post Office, retains a completely clear imprint of my mother – not quite a still, but an episode in slow motion – she was wearing a *cloche* grey felt hat, grey cardigan and a longish grey skirt – the year, 1923 – suddenly toppling over, while holding a cricket bat, as if she had fallen into a pit, I bursting out laughing, my mother very angry, no laughing matter, walking home hobbling, using a cricket stump as a stick, dragging herself all the way up to Mountfield Gardens, I following on a little behind, ashamed of my laughter and trying to keep out of sight; she had sprained her ankle, and could not walk for several days; it wouldn't have happened, but for the cricket lesson.

The amazing thing is that, even after that, they still tried to interest me in the beastly game. A certain spot, again more or less level, between the Linden Park Cricket Ground and the Wellington Rocks remains for ever associated with one of my subterfuges that failed, one of the many times that I was found out. This was three years after the sprained ankle incident. I had made no progress at cricket at my prep school, I *hated* the game, being desperately afraid of being hit by the hard red ball. So my parents had hired some man, encountered somewhere – I suppose there were quite a few such people floating about, taking on odd jobs, in 1926 – to give me an hour's cricket-coaching three times a week, when I came out of school. The first time I put the matter to the man as one adult to another: I did not want to waste an hour fooling about with bat and ball and stumps, I would rather spend it reading. Why not come to an arrangement by which, each time, I gave him his agreed fee – I think it was half-a-crown – and we both then went our ways? He was a reasonable man and accepted my bargain. I did not mind lumbering myself each time with all the implements of our supposed mutual activity. All went well for about three weeks, though, at one week-end, putting me to the test, my father found that I was not making much progress. I should have been warned, but success had made me over-confident. The next time for my lesson, my father turned up, to find no instructor, and myself sitting on a bench, reading a book, with the cricket things laid out on the grass. I was told that I was a liar and a cheat. I don't know what happened to the man; I did not meet him any more, as I had nothing to give him. I did not feel at all guilty. It was just a pity that I had been found out, for the arrangement had served the interests of the man, who got three half-a-crowns a week for doing nothing, merely turning up by the rocks at five; of myself, who got out of a lesson both tiresome and futile; and of my parents, who had had the satisfaction of thinking, for about three weeks, that I was at least making an effort and that I must be overcoming my fear of the hard, swift red ball. I suppose I might have been spared all this, had not my cousin played (as a Gentleman) for Kent. Damn my cousin.

Mountfield Gardens – the fifth or sixth house that we had taken in the two years since we had moved to Tunbridge Wells when I was four – has two further associations, both more pleasant than the episode of the interrupted game. While there, I went to the cinema for the first time, with my mother; we saw *Ben Hur* at the Great Hall, and the chariot race had such a marked effect on me that, every day, as soon as I got back from school, I would practise chariot-racing on the big brown leather armchairs or on the flimsier high-back late-Victorian chairs in inlaid wood with cloth seats. I tilted them sideways onto two legs, even, momentarily, onto one, in order to negotiate corners at break-neck speed, while, with my spare hand, I whipped on my team of horses. It was one of the fairly rare occasions on which I wished that I had a companion. As it was, I had to compete against ten imaginary companions; I generally won, but sometimes I crashed. One of the Victorian chairs was broken in one of the more spectacular crashes. I continued to play the *Ben Hur* game at other addresses, and only gave it up when it became impracticable, once we had furniture of our own. My parents had not worried about the occasional breakages, saying that the furniture in these places was junk anyway and that we paid enough in any case to sit on chairs that were both ugly and uncomfortable. I never entirely abandoned chariot-racing, taking it up again though much out of practice in the far-drawing-room of the Bellevue Royal Hotel, Aberystwyth, competing with my pupils, and, later, on the pale-leather armchairs of Balliol Senior Common Room, in the later stages of Thursday evening guest nights – it would be Friday by then. The only damage to myself I ever sustained, in a long career in this daring and exhilarating sport was a broken left hand, so that I was unable to write for six weeks.

While at Mountfield Gardens, one of my sister's friends from the Godolphin School in Salisbury, Christobel Moore-Molyneux, came to stay at the dark, poky little place; it must have been quite a change from her parents' two houses, the one in London, the other some huge ancestral home in the country; but Chris seemed quite happy with us; perhaps she enjoyed the contrast. My father rose to the occasion rather well. 'Our family portraits', he said, pointing to the dim, leering horrors, staring out of the chocolate gloom – Holman Hunt, 'Bubbles', Grace Darling, King Albert of the Belgians, General Booth – the first time Chris had breakfast with us. The walls of the sitting-room and dining-room, in dark chocolate, were decorated with perhaps the most awful pictures that we had ever encountered in our ever-renewed exploration of furnished lodgings, and goodness knows the four of us must have accumulated an unparalleled exposure to regiments of Monarchs of the Glen, Ann Hathaway's Cottage, the works of Mabel Lucy Attwell, and appalling reproductions of maritime Turners.

There is hardly a location in or around Tunbridge Wells that is not thus associated with some memory or other, most often where I read this or that book: a thatched shelter on the Common, not very far from the Spa Hotel – and designed no doubt as a posting-house for the elderly inmates of that gloomily splendid place – is thus linked with the plays of George Bernard Shaw. *The Rise of the Dutch Republic* was scattered all over the Common, Rusthall and the Happy Valley; but the death of the Hero (my Hero, too) and the Breda scene, 'the little children cried in the streets', took place among the long ferns that edged the eastern curve of the Old Race Course, as I blended my own copious tears with those of the little Dutch children. Or it might be with this or that thought (not pre-cocious or clever ones, just the exciting illuminations of a ten- or a thirteen-year-old). It was the same with itineraries – of these I shall speak later, for the whole area is criss-crossed with them – which I varied to suit various moods: Eridge Park (adventure, exploration), behind Mount Ephraim (enjoyable melancholy), the Hole beyond the black facade (excitement), the lower road to Groombridge (*l'âme slave* – the vegetation was my idea of the Russian steppe), the road to the High Rocks (Gothic gloom), the footpath to Forest Road (Alpine exhilara-tion). From five or six, Tunbridge Wells provided me with a perpetual, self-renewing voyage of discovery of which I never tired: a voyage on which mostly there was but a single traveller. It was an activity I could indulge in generally alone, especially once Kate, my nanny, had left us to get married. My parents must have been either singularly trusting, or they belonged to that generation of middle-class people – especially colonial servants – who were used to leaving their children to amuse themselves and to cope on their own, provided that they turned up for meals and went to bed at the right time. My sister had been left with one of my mother's sisters and brought up with her own children (but not quite *like* one of her own children, she was always made to feel that she was, in some way, a 'poor relation' and that she 'should be grateful') from the age of six weeks till about 5. Certainly, by 6 or 7, I was allowed to roam at will, and made the most of my freedom. At 12, I was given a bicycle, which enabled me to roam even further, often for the best part of a day, taking sandwiches.

3 'SUSSEX VIEW'

Although childhood is often said to be dominated by fear – Graham Greene says something of the kind – I cannot say that this was the case with mine. I was not particularly afraid of anyone or anything (dogs, of course, excepted) on the Common, not even of the Highland 'flasher', who seemed to have camped somewhere in the Tropical Rainforest, and who used to emerge suddenly from the bushes, pulling up his kilt, when my friends and I were taking the short cut on our way to or from Rose Hill. He seemed more comical than frightening: and when he shouted at us, it was in a funny accent which we could not understand. We did not need the grown-ups to tell us that he was harmless, we could see that for ourselves; they would add 'shell-shock' or something of the kind (a portmanteau expression in the vocabulary in use in the twenties that covered a multitude of eccentricities manifested by adult males); we just thought that he was a funny man in funny clothes. I was however, very much afraid of thunderstorms, and there used to be terrible ones, flashing and rumbling from the direction of Tonbridge and the Medway Valley, so that even the thick-drawn curtains would not keep the great flashes from lighting up my bedroom as I lay quivering with terror. I may be wrong, but the summers of the first half of the twenties seem to have been hot, sticky, and thundery, and, in Cumberland Gardens, my nights were often haunted by the bells of fire-engines, as they tried to put out the fires that kept on breaking out among the brown ferns and undergrowth of the Common. I was also very frightened of the sound, at night, of the roundabouts and shooting-stalls on the fairground near Major York's Road, because I knew that the fair would bring in all sorts of alarming people from High Brooms and Hawkenbury to the bottom end of the Common, almost within sight of my bedroom in Cumberland Walk (earlier, I had actually lived *on* the Common, in a black clapboard cottage called Fonthill, and very near to the fairground, but then I slept in my mother's bed and felt quite safe). The fair was always in August, always *the* month of fear, because high summer brought out the violent people, the half-naked, hairy-chested people, the tattooed people, the trippers, the couples lying on top of one another on the Common; it was the month when wars broke out and when there were thunderstorms. Sometimes, in the hot August nights, I would be woken up by the shouts and untuneful singing of drunken people as they staggered up Mount Sion, as if about to storm those middle-class heights. Would they turn off into Cumberland Walk? I lay in bed, sweating with fear and August sultriness. But Mount Sion would soon be plunged once more in reassuring silence, broken, now and then, by the sound of a car as it changed gear. I knew about that; danger would not come from a car, only from the sound of many feet, walking, or, worse, running. Later, after we had made what turned out to be our final move, in over a score of moves, as I lay with my feet towards Birdcage Walk, with the Italianate cream-coloured house by the double archway gleaming in the soft gaslight, the same sound, coming from the equally steep Grove Hill, would send me off on the first stage towards sleep. There was something very romantic and mysterious about people who thus drove through the night. Where had they been? Where were they going? I would turn over, and fall fast asleep.

I had regular August nightmares about being savaged, even eaten, by enormous black dogs (no nightmares, really, for, by 14, I had already been bitten a dozen times, mostly by very small white dogs), and, all the year round, about failing to complete my homework. In the spare room at my naval uncle's in Southsea, my bed faced onto a large picture depicting the death of Nelson on one of the darker decks of the *Victory*. The recumbent Nelson was in the centre of the composition and all the light seemed to concentrate on his livid, dying face. The picture both terrified me and made me cry; my female cousins, no doubt used to Nelson, thought that I was a cry-baby. The scene was bad enough by daylight, but, in the dark, Nelson's pale face and scattered white hair recurred in dream after dream, and I remember waking up screaming: the 'face' had come right up close to me, and my aunt, in a long woollen nighty covered in bobbles, had come into my room to see what was the matter.

Normally, I was not afraid of the dark; for that matter, I seldom experienced it, the town being well lit by the soft, sighing gas-lamps. But once, when I was 12, I was out very late, and took a short cut through a small wood just as the light was failing. In the dark, every sound, every rustle, every crack of a branch under my feet caused in me a mounting panic, so that I broke into a blind run, tripping up, my feet and trousers catching in the undergrowth; every time I stopped, I thought I heard the sound of footsteps and heavy breathing behind me. I was frightened out of my wits, and enormously relieved when I reached the familiar stile which led onto the road to Hawkenbury. I did not try any more night-walking through dark woods after that.

I was always afraid of High Brooms and of the people who lived there, and I was rather afraid of the upper reaches of

Upper Grosvenor Road, though, at 12, I summoned up enough
courage to penetrate it *almost* to the bottom. I was absolutely
terrified of the noisy, rough, ill-spoken boys of King Charles
Choir School. I knew about them, for, at one time, we lived in a
house called Sussex View, and the view of Sussex we enjoyed –
if that is the right word – was of the mean, parsimonious-
looking Church of England school in wretched yellowish and
pinkish lavatory brick. The alarming school was just the other
(Sussex) side of the Walk. No wonder we did not have to pay a
very high rent for the lease of Sussex View, no wonder there was
such a rapid turnover of embattled middle-class tenants, with
such a *vis-à-vis*. By a small act of mercy, the entrance to Sussex
View was placed at right angles to the house, that is, onto the
Gardens, rather than onto the perilously exposed Walk, so that,
taking a quick survey of the enemy stronghold, I could make a
rapid exit through the gate, bolt up the Gardens, turning right
into what I knew was the relative safety of Chapel Place, from
where, half-concealed by the wall in front of the Baptist chapel,
I could watch out for the running, shouting mob, as, swinging
their satchels on the end of their straps, so as to hit one another,
they emerged from the front of King Charles, to disappear
almost immediately down the London Road, spreading terror
all the way along Vale Road, Mount Pleasant and the Five
Ways, until they were engulfed in the unknown areas beyond
Goods Station Road. I would have made a detour of several
miles, rather than risk meeting them head on and face to face.
The point of maximum danger was beneath the enormous pair
of spectacles, each containing a glaucous, staring, and rather
alarming blue eye surrounded by an even more alarming white
that hung over the shop of Mr Bateman, the optician. It was not
till I was about 16 that I could pass under the 'eyes' without a
feeling of sickening apprehension, and prepared to make a bolt
for it, in any direction that would take me away from the front
of the howling, whistling, cat-calling, jeering mob. I did not
know what I had done to earn such intense hostility – perhaps it

was my clothing, or my appearance, or because I was wearing the wrong sort of cap. I was afraid they would knock me down or stone me. Once, when suddenly coming upon the dreaded black and yellow caps, at a time when they should have been back in their lairs, I took to my heels, rushing through the traffic at the bottom of Frant Road, streaked through the Pantiles, and only stopped running at the level of the Orange Tea Rooms, where I was recognised by three of my mother's friends, who asked me why I looked so hot. At least there I was *safe*. When we lived in Sussex View, I was 5 or 6. All I knew about the French Revolution was from *The Tale of Two Cities*, read to me in my grandmother's drawing-room in the Hythe. I did not know anything about the Russian Revolution, though there were flag-days and collections in King Charles for the Relief of the Famine in the Ukraine. But I certainly *did* know about class antagonism and class fear.

In Tunbridge Wells, 'Sussex' was all right to be *viewed*, as long as the view was not that of the hateful choir school. But 'Sussex' had rather a bad name in other ways. Later, especially during the War, which brought to the town an increase of population not all welcome to the respectable elements of the resident middle-classes, it became associated with a public house, down a discreet alley-way that led off from behind the Pantiles and that would be missed by most tourists and, by a good many residents. It was called 'The Sussex Shades'. The name was appropriate, for it was (just) in Sussex and it tended to be frequented by rather shady-looking characters who looked as though they belonged to some secret brotherhood or sisterhood and who had made their way there in response to a password not readily communicated. The interior of the Lounge Bar was always dark, the pub being enclosed among taller buildings. The landlord, a red-faced man, his very black hair plastered down and parted in the middle, wore a striped waistcoat and a heavy signet ring on one of the fingers of his left hand. There was a curious torpor about the place, not a peaceful quiet, such as one encountered in the Grove Tavern, where the landlord, the landlady and the regulars always seemed half-asleep, coming to life with rather startled expressions when a customer opened the door into the tiny bar, but more an air of expectancy, as if waiting for something to happen. It was quiet, but not relaxed. There were always half-a-dozen youngish women, brash, in strident green, red, or pink sheen dresses, sitting smoking on high stools at the bar. From the summer of 1940 to that of 1944, there were always a few young officers from South-Eastern Command, their swagger-sticks on the tables at which they were sitting, drinking shorts. At other tables – but never coalescing with the uniformed customers – were young men fresh from Guy's Dental School, which had been evacuated to the town. The two groups eyed one another, listlessly, but without hostility, with one eye on the bar, and one eye on the door. After some time, during which everyone seemed to be frozen in their assigned positions, one of the girls would slowly climb down from her high perch, taking care not to trip, and go and sit at one of the tables occupied by the uniformed figures. Then one of the dental students, standing at the bar to order a round of pints of bitter, would engage in a whispered conversation with the girl in the livid green dress, following which she would abandon her perch and go and sit among the dentists-to-be in their corner at a distance from the officers. In due course, as if in response to a series of secret signals, the other girls – pink, purple, lavender, electric blue, puce – would likewise step down with slow deliberation, smoothing their brilliant dresses at the knees, and go and sit each at a different masculine table. Conversations would remain restrained, almost confidential, no coarse jokes, no communication from table to table. The landlord looked on, very still, his face completely empty. One or two more masculine customers would come in, look around, and nod at this group or that, followed by three more girls who arrived together and took up positions on the empty bar-stools. The

33

Sussex Shades had a sort of *louche* intimacy, quite unlike the ambience of any of the other pubs in the town. It was hard to put your finger on it, but you felt that things were not quite right. It had something to do with the War, a period during which the Shades discreetly prospered. When the War was over, the place suddenly closed, remaining so for several weeks, when it reopened under new management. It was not the same at all; the landlord with the wide, imperturbable boxer's face, the officers, the dental students, and the brightly coloured girls had all gone, to be replaced by rather broken-down old men who sucked their unlit pipes and elderly women in hats. Sussex had recovered its respectability, and the Pantiles had lost the slight *frisson* of vice.

4 LITTLE MOUNT SION

I suggested, at the beginning of the section devoted to approaches to the town, that the back-to-front station offered a suitable introduction to a place that contained many bizarreries, and, for the observer who pushed up the steep little cobbled streets, many small, rather engaging objects of surprise, wonder, and delight. At the top of Little Mount Sion stood a little white cottage called Swan Cottage, suitably guarded by a stone swan, and with a ring attached to a heavy black chain round its neck. If I had accompanied my mother on shopping-and-stopping in the High Street and the expedition had been completed, I would propose: 'Let's go home by the swan'. It was not just the swan that recommended to me that particular itinerary, there were other attractions: just beyond the swan, there was a tiny shop-window painted a deep green, and marked, in white letters: Engineer. In the window was some sort of engine: cog-wheels, ball-bearings, a thickly-greased piston, a mysterious object the presence of which suggested that of even more mysterious objects inside. The shop was very dark, so that one could not see in. It also seemed to be permanently closed: in the course of years I never saw anyone go in and come out, or the green door open. But the machine and the white letters remained in place, though none of the many people I asked had ever *seen* the Engineer or knew who he was. I thought of him as a man of mystery, who worked only at night – and, on one occasion, when I was in my thirties, and was leaving the Compasses after closing-time, I did actually see a bright, hard light coming from the little low green shop. But it was the only occasion that I did, though I went to the pub opposite almost every night. As a child, I came to the conclusion that the Engineer was a Mad Inventor, who only worked while everyone else slept. I did not then know about Infernal Machines; even if I had, I would never have associated one of my favourite areas of the town – or indeed *any* area of the town save the *zone interdite* surrounding the dreadful choir school – with violence, cruelty and unkindness. I was always glad to see the silent, immobile, crouching, well-greased machine in its rightful place. I liked objects to be where they had always been for thus they contributed to giving my childhood and adolescence the immensely reassuring sense of continuity. The swan and the machine, like the little stone archers seated on their little stone crocodiles at the entrance to Camden Park, stood on guard against change and disaster and protected me from violence, war and revolution.

Near the green and white Engineer was a tiny sweetshop with even tinier bow-windows, and huge jars of coloured gob-stoppers (that changed colour several times as one sucked through them), displayed among tins of snuff, cigarette-rollers and Rizla paper, kept by an old woman who looked and dressed like the be-spectacled sheep in *Alice through the Looking Glass*. She also sold the *Kent & Sussex Courier* and the *Advertiser* (stolid guardians of continuity, the former respectable, the latter less so), no national dailies. What would they have been doing in this lilliput enclave of peaceful provincialism?

Further along, a small butcher's-shop had an elaborate painted sheep, in washable coloured tiles, surrounded by a floral design, on its lower front. Staring from the top of the canopy, which also bore the name of the butcher in coloured letters that seemed to be sprouting leaves and foliage at their extremities, but which also looked as if they were eatable, was the porcelain head of a pig, like a secular gargoyle, dead centre, very pink in the face, and with very blue eyes, not at all unlike those of some of my mother's tweed-and-jaeger-clad spinster friends, and equally innocent and vacant. The tiled sheep was in profile and faced towards the swan; but the pig's head seemed to be in the process of reproducing itself in the neat rows of several heads that looked out of the window of the shop, a sort of porker kindergarten on a cheerful outing, beneath the rabbits and hares, pheasants and turkeys, hanging from hooks. It was a bright, cheerful little shop that looked as if it were made of marzipan and that in the summer was protected by an awning in blue and white stripes.

Next to the sweet-shop stood, on the one side, the minute Grove Tavern, in yellow clapboard, surely the smallest pub in Tunbridge Wells, and, on the other, a little corrugated-iron shed painted cream, with a roof painted red, and that belonged to Toe H, with a flame coming out of a saucer painted on its front. Like the 'Engineer', it always seemed to be shut. Perhaps, such was the competition in the town of seven hills and many chapels, it had lapsed, or maybe it held services at odd hours of the night. Beyond Toe H, a wooden cottage with steep steps leading up to the doorway set at the side, not the front, had a diminutive rock-garden decorated with gnomes, stone rabbits, a windmill, a fortified castle (a miniature Bodiam Castle painted bright red), a watermill, a pair of stone cannon and a tiny well with real water inside. It was the sort of house that should have been inhabited by the dwarfs who ran the Nevill Bakery; but, in fact, they lived in Cumberland Gardens, where they had special steps and a tiny staircase put in.

In this area, situated between the top of Little Mount Sion and one of the entrances to the Grove, everything was to scale, though the swan was almost as tall as the white cottage that it guarded. It had the unity of diminutiveness, a sort of Toy Tunbridge Wells, though the inhabitants were of normal size and seemed to be much too big for their shops. The sheep-lady, for instance, appeared to be completely hemmed in in the tiny downstairs room. Getting in and out, without upsetting or breaking anything, must have been a delicate and laborious business, involving the displacement of walls of jars and their subsequent re-erection. This was only supposition, for I never saw the sheep-lady move at all, she was always installed behind the counter, sitting in the half-light. Even more formidable to negotiate was the doll-like corkscrew staircase that led from the back of the shop to the tiny single-room above, where the sheep-lady presumably slept. The red-faced butcher and his son also looked much too large for their edible shop, although their movements were nimble and easy.

Little Mount Sion had earned its name. It was much smaller, humbler, more secretive, than its big brother, Mount Sion, which had little to offer, save a stamp-shop near the bottom, and my aunt's hospital, half-way up, where I could replenish my stocks of glass eyes and ether, thanks to my special relationship with the dispenser.

5 GROVE HILL

Grove Hill, later Grove Hill Road, another way up to my home, on the contrary, had a great *deal* to offer, starting from the one-storeyed wooden shop – little more than a shed, with a flat roof covered over in some sort of tarpaulin – of R. Septimus Gardiner, Taxidermist, his window displaying his skills: red squirrels on their hind-legs eating nuts against a background of branches and foliage; sinister-looking pike, with whisky-drinking eyes, submarine colours and scales, the Terror of the Deep, lurking against a background of yellowing rushes and trailing pale green river-weeds; a woodcock with little glass eyes – R. Septimus Gardiner took a great deal of trouble over eyes; a gaggle of humming-birds on little branches and protected within a house made of white shell, artificially ruined, like a Salvador Dali palace; a yellow-eyed buzzard against a background of cloud and threatening sky; congeries of owls, in all shapes and sizes, and facing all sorts of ways, rather crowded, and all in the same glass-fronted box: recalling those group-caricatures, of musicians, poets, actors, politicians, novelists, a varying display of hair, beards, collars, spectacles, stocks, of the eighteen-sixties *Charivari*, or the Victorian equivalent; stuffed foxes, stoats, badgers, weasels, dogs – for once silent and harmless and acceptable, like the dog with a money-box on its back that used to reside, in its case, on Portsmouth Marine or Central – cats, lizards, even bats. The shop was so shallow that the taxidermist had to work right up against the window, surrounded by his beady-eyed master-pieces, as if they were anxious to find out about the identity of the newcomer to the club, just as, from outside, and having placed my satchel on the ground, I sometimes watched the dedicated artist at work. He never looked up, but must have been aware of my presence, my face right up against the glass, at the level of the top of his head, and, a few years later, well above it. He was a balding, rather scruffy man, with a lot of dandruff on his shoulders, and a check waistcoat, with two buttons missing, and that did not match his coat. He did not look at all prosperous, but I think he did quite well. All the inhabitants of his cases had been done to order. Of course, his confined premises must have imposed an upper limit on the full range available to him. He could only do small animals and fish; the big beasts would not have fitted in, so that cheetahs, pumas, tigers, and all the big cats were denied even a temporary residence on Grove Hill. I thought his long, shallow, single-storeyed, glass fronted shop looked like an enlargement of one of the many cases. It would have been appropriate if, when the time came, his own remains should have been stuffed and preserved immobilised in the midst of his many triumphs. He was a kind and gentle creature, and an artist in small things, a committed miniaturist. Alas! his little shed-shop was pulled down years ago. I don't know what became of him, perhaps orders ran out as fashions changed. For, already in the mid-thirties, when I was an undergraduate at Oxford, I used to talk regularly to an elderly man who occupied the seat below the bastion of the city wall in Merton gardens, (on sunny days it was an ideal sun-spot); he, too, it appeared from his conversation, which was quiet and without a trace of bitterness, had seen better days, when he had filled the common rooms of half the male colleges with great rearing beasts; it was the *War*, he said, that had killed off the demand. Happily, I still possess two examples of the work of the seventh Gardiner: a stuffed woodcock, and a stuffed white partridge, inherited from my grandfather, and a reminder of one of my favourite stopping-places on the way up the steep hill.

One down from the taxidermist's was another wooden shack-shop, equally shallow, and painted, like a gypsy caravan, in bright green and scarlet, picked out with yellow piping, with the name 'Love, Fruit & Vegetables', in flowing yellow letters with black edges on one side to give them relief. The likeness was probably not entirely fortuitous, for old Mr Love and his son had blue-black hair and very bright dark eyes.

Young Mr Love had married my nanny, Kate Scurrell, after courting her for some time, standing up in his little wooden cart and talking to her at night through her bedroom window, invitingly open, and which faced onto a lane that ran behind the house in Cumberland Gardens. My mother had declared herself distressed at the *mésalliance*, saying that Kate, a very literate girl, had deserved something better. It might have been so, but it would be hard to reach any formal conclusion. Kate was a no doubt typical example of the borrowed mobility, like the borrowed accent, of the domestic servant. She was a typical hybrid nanny, wrenched out of her native Essex and her extensive, and no doubt loving, Scurrell relatives (still thick on the ground in North Essex and South Suffolk) and put down in Kent, a deportation at first sight brutal and unfeeling. But perhaps one should not exaggerate the attachment to birthplace and to kin felt by members of the landless rural population in the nineteen-hundreds and the nineteen-twenties. Ronald Blythe has suggested that the men were willing enough to exchange the land and Suffolk for the hazards of the Boer War and the adventure of August 1914 with hardly a pang. So was this such a cruel thing? What *was* there, in Great Holland or Little Holland, or Thorpe-le-Soken, for the seventh or the eighth child – and a daughter at that – of a small farmer from the Hundred of Tendring? Surely Tunbridge Wells offered better prospects than Clacton-on-Sea, better even than middle-class Frinton? Was it just exploitation? If so, it was readily accepted. And a nanny was not *quite* a servant; the longer Kate stayed with us, the posher and the more ladylike became her accent. She had already been literate, making the most of the little a Church of England school in Great Holland would have to offer. But being a nanny-cum-general-maid was a sort of education, too. She taught me my letters and my numerals, and, in doing so, she may have picked up something *au passage*. She read to me a great deal – rather more than my mother did – and some of this – Dickens especially – must have rubbed off on her own retentive mind. By the time she got married – in 1924 or 1925 – it must have seemed to her that her opportunities were running out; if she had come to us at 18 or 19, replacing my sister's nanny, Rose, who had died of Spanish influenza, in 1919, she would then have been heading for 26 or 27, and may have felt inclined to take on the first firm offer. There had been others. I had been aware of a khaki presence, or of *several* khaki presences, as a sort of blurr at eye-level beside

my pram and moving along with it, in 1919 and 1920, both in
Frinton, and, above all, in Colchester (where there was an
abundance of that pungent colour), but khaki would have no
serious appeal to a farmer's daughter, who, coming from North
Essex, would know about soldiers in any case. There had been
others – not in khaki, but in dark blue suits with red faces – but
it was hard to know whether they had been well-intentioned
'followers' – they may have been just on the look-out for any
easy pick-up on the Common – and this was certainly one of the
functions of the Common, though not one of which I would
have been especially aware. I was knowing enough, however,
never to mention the regular appearance of the red men in blue
– one even had a name, he was called Nick – to my mother, on
returning from the walks with Kate. There grew between Kate
and myself an undefined, yet aware, complicity.

Kate was an ambivalent being in every way, not part of the
family, yet very much *of* the family. Her affection for myself
was genuine, and so was her rather embarrassing gush, as if she
had been grateful for her association with my early fortunes and
misfortunes. She had been the first in the field as far as I was
concerned, was irreplaceable, and indeed, was never replaced,
so that I went on belonging to her, in a number of unstated, but
mutually understood, ways, long after she had changed her
status, and become Mrs Love. It sounds rather monstrous, but
I think she was prouder of me – and of 'Miss Diana' (I remained
'Richard') than of her own children, whom she tried,
pathetically no doubt, but again quite sincerely, to model on us.
Kate was ambitious as well as deferential – a combination
common enough in the blurred and ambivalent hierarchies of
domesticity and semi-domesticity. Had she held on, she might
have been promoted to the dubious rank of 'companion' or of
governess, her purely domestic duties being delegated to a
daily. I have no doubt that all this was put to her – perhaps not
in so many words, but by hints and allusions – by my mother
when her engagement to Love was being debated; and of that

debate even I was aware. For Kate herself, it must have been a matter of fine calculation. Certainly she did not rush into marriage, as certainly, she was unhappy to leave us – indeed, for years and years, she endeavoured in every way to cling on to us, enquiring of our health, our schooling, our achievements (she was too intelligent to enquire about our failures), and still attempting in many ways to live through us, perhaps also as an escape from what turned out to be the rather sordid realities of greengrocery at the Love level.

Such relations are very difficult to write about, if only because *one* of the parties will never be completely candid, even with herself, and will above all *never* write about them. So we have to make do with the childrens' view of them, and this, like a child's sense of size, space, height, or distance, will always be wildly out of proportion, though, like a magnifying-glass, bringing out the detail (what I most remember of Kate is the worry and anxiety that always seemed to be in her eyes, also the fragile bones that stood out in her very thin neck). Certainly, my knowledge of and my affection for Kate made me early aware of the sheer complication of relations that hovered on the borderlines of class and personal. Indeed, to my eyes, Kate could not be categorised at all in terms of class; she was classless because she was Kate, not Mrs Love, or the former Miss Scurrell – a form of address denied her by her semi-domestic status though I am sure that she much preferred to be the more familiar Kate. There was in fact nothing insulting about the regular use of the Christian name, and had she been a *real* servant, she would have been addressed as 'Scurrell'. Kate was very important to me, too, in quite a different way. She represented the continuity between Frinton, Colchester, and Tunbridge Wells, she carried with her to the Kent and Sussex border something of her own and my own native Hundred of Tendring; even the Essex twang survived, intermittently breaking through the careful overlay of middle-class speech, as mirrored, and slightly distorted, from the kitchen and nursery.

Kate never had meals with us (save during picnics on the beach, when such niceties were abandoned – she could hardly have sat apart, eating on her own, a few yards away, in an imaginary kitchen), yet she knew me much better, indeed knew much more *about me* – including my guilty secrets (and I always had quite a few of these) than anyone who *did* have meals with us. At this period, it was my mother, rather than her substitute and stand-in, Kate, who appeared to me somehow at one remove. When Kate went, I was just left that much more on my own. I don't think I minded this, for I always found plenty to occupy me and plenty to observe; but I had lost a companion and an accomplice, and never found another one so close.

Where my mother stood in all this I cannot judge; all I know is that she thought that Kate was making a big mistake, was not 'making the best of herself', and that her family would not have approved of Love and would have been aghast at the thought of her marrying a gypsy (it was typical of Kate's desperate concern for the genteel that she always flew in the face of evidence and denied that Love *was* a gypsy – she may even have managed to convince herself of this article of faith, such was her overriding preoccupation with what was deemed to be 'proper', her only luxury, her only form of wealth). My mother was quite sincere in her adopted rôle of *in loco parentis*; she felt an obligation to Kate's parents and elder brothers, because they were 'respectable people' and because she had been able to assure them that she was going into a 'good home'. She may also have found it an awful nuisance getting along without Kate, or, at least, the prospect of having to do so, because I don't think Kate's departure actually weighed at all heavily on her leisure activities and social engagements. Of course, my mother was right in her warning; she was generally right in such matters. She had an annoying habit of being able to spot impending disaster well ahead. 'I never liked the woman from the moment I first set eyes on her, though Frank [my father] found her charming with her red hair and blue eyes,' she would say, in the consciousness of

43

having been right from the start. She was speaking, of the mother of one of my Dublin friends in my house at Shrewsbury, who later murdered her, throwing her body over a cliff. This was several years later. Certainly, poor Kate went downhill pretty fast after her marriage, soon moving from the rented rooms crammed with new furniture on H. P., off the Grove (Meadow Hill Road, I think) to a slum cottage, in a small line of slum cottages, all of them sharing a single pump, all very dark and damp, and all discreetly hidden from view by the big *Kent & Sussex Courier* (Kate called it the 'Currier') building and Weekes' ultra-respectable emporium, a suppurating slum within a few yards of the Central Station, the existence of which I was one of the few people – apart from old Mr Weekes, who owned the row of cottages – to know about.

Unlike my mother, I had at once approved of the match, for Love Junior used to take me for rides in his cart – also painted in red and green, with yellow piping and with a heart-shaped board at the back announcing name and trade. He was a friendly chap, always laughing and whistling and I loved bowling along beside him, sitting on the low green bench, and holding on with my hands, behind his little piebald horse, as we careered down the steep incline of Grove Hill, sparks flying from the iron-lined wheels, like Ben Hur. Indeed, Love Senior and Junior both had something in common with Mills, my grandfather's groom in Colchester; they drank a great deal, both in the pubs off Monson Road, after they had attended the vegetable market, in those on the Pembury Road, including a big one called, I think, the Gun, and then the Kentish Yeoman, conveniently opposite the shop – customers who knew the habits of the pair and who wanted to buy something, would seek them out in the public bar there; but their frequent absences lost them a great deal of female middle-class trade. I could hardly imagine my mother and her friends looking for them in the noisy, smoky Yeoman. My mother, at least, after one or two such experiences, transferred her custom to the respectable

Garling & Scott's, very deferential people further up the hill. She had, she claimed, given the Loves a try 'in order to help Kate'. What she did not say was that the Loves were much cheaper, and their fruit and vegetables fresher, than Garling & Scott's.

Sometimes, both Loves failed to make it even to the Yeoman, the driverless cart hurtling down Grove Hill signalling to the more experienced observers that father and son had got stuck, not together, for they had their own individual ports of call and were not in the habit of drinking together (save at the Yeoman), at earlier stages of their progress from the market. But the piebald horse always managed to stop exactly at the level of the shop. Much later on, Love Senior or Love Junior would appear at the top of Grove Hill – never walking together – zig-zagging and guiding themselves down, like mountaineers on ropes, from lamp-post to lamp-post. Old Mr Love fell out of his cart a number of times; his son had a firmer grasp, and I have seen him going down the hill, in ever widening curves, driving standing up, the whip in his hand, and letting out loud whoops. They certainly lent a bit of colour – literally and morally – to the rather drab respectability of Grove Hill. In the end, they had to sell out. The old man lingered on, in the tiny house behind the *Courier*. Kate's husband often took to the road – perhaps he really was a romany – leaving Kate with three small children, one named after me, and one after my aunt, Kathleen, whose gushing speech and genteel mannerisms Kate very much admired. I have often wondered what happened to Richard Love, and his elder brother, Maurice. I gathered that, at least, they were wise enough to have survived the War – their father and their grandfather would have approved of that. Kate herself looked 50 at 35, 60 at 40. To make ends meet, she had to take up odd jobs as a cleaner, a char, or an occasional cook: a sad and humiliating social decline for one so genuinely ladylike, so intelligent and so literate. When my mother died, I asked Kate, who was then living on a new Council estate, what she would like in memory of her; she said: a silver teapot. So every time I went to see her she would insist on giving me Lapsang tea from it. By then she was looking increasingly haggard and grey, her hair thinning on the top, and with lines of care around her intelligent grey eyes, her speech still exaggeratedly ladylike and still with flashes of the old Essex, now a dull monotone, the voice of utter resignation and defeat, as if all the stuffing had been knocked out of her. She followed my career, academic and otherwise, with extreme attention and embarrassing possess-iveness, with remarks such as: 'How proud your mother would be of you now!' Perhaps she would have been, but, thank goodness, she would never have shown it. Kate certainly was. I was still furnishing her with some sort of a substitute life, though I am glad to say that her own children, in their various successes, good careers, happy and suitable marriages, gave her a great deal of satisfaction in her own right, as they should have done. Though, in her sixties, Kate looked as thin and as frail as my mother in her eighties, she herself lived on well into her own eighties, the old Essex toughness reasserting itself beneath the appearance of fragility and after over sixty years of exile from the flat, windy coast.

I have lingered on the subject of Kate because she was so much the link between our many moves, in Frinton, then in Tunbridge Wells, so much so that, even after she left us, it was to go only just down the road, that is to the bottom of Grove Hill, a descent symbolic of her own social decline, so that, for years, she remained part of the familiar Grove Hill topography. I could take in her slum cottage, just as I could take in the Loves' shop, the taxidermist's, on my way back from school, or, if I went another way, via Mount Pleasant and the Calverley Road, I could take in the big grocer's shop near the Kosmos cinema. The grocer would sometimes give me little booklets – advertisements for Bisto – the brightly coloured pages of which, if flicked with a steady movement from the top, would give the appearance of animation, like a film run fast: a man jumping, a dog running, a horse going over an obstacle, a master caning a boy, a woman smacking a child on her lap, that I would set in action on the way home, becoming so absorbed in the coloured movement that I would even miss the artificial eyes in the window of the oculist (who supplied them to my aunt's hospital), would walk into a lamp-post, or would catch my foot in the roots of one of the cedars that stood in the bowl of the short-cut across Calverley Park. The booklets were well worth the occasional detour, though it would mean sacrificing the varied pleasures offered by Grove Hill, including my weekly copy of *Modern Boy* (I was not very modern, but I craved after the tin-embossed flat models of Malcolm Campbell's racing car or of the blue-painted seaplane in the Schneider Trophy that were given away free with certain numbers and that I would feel for as soon as I got my copy) waiting for me, every Wednesday, at the newsagent half-way up on the left.

There was another wooden shack-shop even further up the hill, and also on the left. It was even smaller and flimsier than the taxidermist's and the Loves' bright bazaar. Painted in a drab and sober green, it was occupied by a watchmaker jeweller, who could generally be seen, wearing a white tennis eyeshade, and with a magnifying glass screwed into his eye. I don't know what sort of jewellery he dealt in; perhaps he just did repairs. The window displayed an array of cheap alarm-clocks, some of them with coloured pictures on their dials, or even eyes and mouths, and watches that may, or may not, have been cheap, but which all went and all marked the same time: generally 5.20, when I went past with my school-bag on my way home.

There was not much more of interest on that side of the hill: the big doors to the depot in which Mr Weekes' hearses were kept (for that emporium dealt in respectable death as well as in tasteful, but unostentatious life, clothes, fabrics, carpets, cretonnes and chintzes) forbiddingly closed, as if in homage to the discretion of 'passing away', though I did once see a black hearse being trundled out and two horses attached to it. I

47

always crossed the road, so as not to pass the closed doors within touching distance; it seemed safer to have the width of the road between them and myself. There was not much more of interest on *that* side of the hill, though I was intrigued by the small hall in green corrugated-iron which stood, near the Yeoman (but disassociating itself from the Yeoman), on the other side, and that served the Pentecostal Brethren, one of the many sects that thrived in the town. Where it drew its congregation from I did not know, but it hardly seemed to belong to Grove Hill, especially at its lower end, amidst the amiable anarchy of the Loves and the animal mummies of the seventh-born.

6 MY MOTHER'S HOUSE

Our own house – the twentieth or so leased, but, as it turned out, of uncharacteristic duration, as if my parents had at last tired of the charms of moving every three months, with the help of the 'Outside Porter', a man with a self-designed red-topped cap who stood with his red hand-cart outside the Central Station – fully conformed to the unstated prescriptions that governed so many of the oddities of the town, starting, as if in warning of what to expect beyond, from the back-to-front, tunnel-bound station. The house, too, was back-to-front. Its actual address was 5a Grove Hill but it faced onto Claremont Road, and was reached by a long, outside stone staircase, giving the rather stark facade some of the grim appearance of the *Karl Marx Hof* in Vienna, though it was grey, and not a bilious beige like the latter. It was certainly designed to show off the worse side first. The houses, a pretty crescent of Regency buildings facing onto Birdcage Walk and a small park covered with overgrown rhododendron bushes (the site of my attempted seduction by a blue-suited, furtive, heavy-breathing man when I was 12) and silver-birch, had been divided into upper and lower flats (maisonnettes was the word used by the estate-agents), two storeys each. The lower flats led straight out onto the little park and Birdcage Walk, so that their curving fronts really *were* fronts. The upper flats had no direct access to the Walk, to which, as part of a planned ensemble, they rightly belonged, so that they were also excluded from the little park that went with it, though their handsome wrought-iron balconies gave a much better view of it than that enjoyed by the flats below. It was an instance of a pretty slipshod conversion that had been carried out some time in the early twenties. The steps commanded the only means of entry, so there was no secondary escape route, no back door, with the result that the house could indeed be a trap, in case of disturbance or revolution. I felt that this disadvantage was partly offset by the advantage offered by a superior height. We were a long way from the ground, and so less exposed to the sudden rage of a mob determined to break in than the lower flats at ground level. Certainly, I appreciated the security offered by the height of the building, much that I regretted the absence of a means of rapid escape. All one could do would be to go up higher. On the other hand, thanks to the steps – there were twenty-five of them – one had plenty of time to observe the approach of any sinister-looking, dark stranger, commissar, brown-shirt or Kentish *septembriseur*. All things considered, it was about as safe a haven as one could hope for, though I would have been happier if there had been access to the roof and thence to neighbouring houses in the crescent. At one time, preoccupied with such fears, I contemplated keeping a rope-ladder in my work-room, but I was uncertain where to obtain such a device. I did not know of any shop that specialised in rope-ladders. The middle classes were perhaps displaying over-confidence, something that I for one did not share. It was not *fire* that I was afraid of, but *people*; or fire lit by people. As it turned out, the one time I really *was* in danger, I was caught *outside* the house, not *in* it; I could see, from well down Claremont Road, the large, red-faced policeman standing halfway up the steps; but as I had nowhere to go and hide in – Percy House, the home of my sister's in-laws, did occur to me, but I at once rejected the idea – I walked towards the steps and the danger that I could not avoid. It was not a very terrible danger, in any case; and, much that I knew every footpath and every back passage of the Royal Borough, I could not see myself on the run and living rough.

The interior of the house dutifully echoed back some of the back-to-front themes proclaimed to street and park. The dining-room could only be reached through the kitchen. But the box-room, on the top storey (the second of the flat, and so the fourth of the original house) led out onto a flat roof protected by a low wall, so that it was quite safe; and that commanded a magnificent view of Mount Ephraim along most of its length. So did the French windows of the drawing-room which opened onto the curving balcony. Thus the upper flats, though ostensibly penalised – no back door, a confusing address, access to a banal road rather than to the secluded little park – enjoyed in fact considerable advantages; and, as eating takes such a very small part in English sociability (our meals were taken at speed, as if we were all in a rush to get back to the drawing-room side of the house, which also included my work-room, provided with a small, but very effective fireplace) it did not matter that the dining-room was so poky, was overlooked by everyone on the way to the front-door, and seemed but an extension of the kitchen, itself little more than a narrow corridor. All the ugliest bits of furniture were relegated to the dining-room. When my mother and I were alone in the house, we generally had the evening meal in the drawing-room, at a small round table in the window; and, in good weather, we had tea on the balcony, and breakfast on the flat roof. My bedroom was also on the side facing the rhododendron and lilac bushes and the little park. It was very quiet, and gave a feeling of complete security. At night, from my bed, I could see the line of pale lights marking out Mount Ephraim, and, if I got up, the two arches, white and ghostly in the soft gaslight at the entry to

Birdcage Walk. I woke up to the sight of the top of a silver-birch, as it stirred lazily in the wind, of the white-fronted Wellington, the red Earl's Court, and the tower of Rusthall church; and sometimes I woke up to a white blankness, like a mass of still cotton-wool, beyond the curving window; the fog that blocked out all traces of the town and that rose up from the level of the High Street, or hanging in trails over the dark trees, revealing dimly the two arches. The only sound would be that of feet and of wheels proceeding along the walk towards the other two arches and the Grove. The bedroom was as intimate as it was secure; I had occupied it ever since my sister's marriage, and I felt no fears there. I knew all the objects in it and the titles and positions of all the books in the book-cases: Anthony a Wood on the round table by the bed, a couple of Strindberg plays, Sean O'Casey's *The Silver Tassie*, an illustrated Gauguin, some Dostoevsky and Turgenev in French translation, none save the wonderfully malicious à Wood, regular reading, but each kept in its place, because it had always been there, or for as long as I could remember. They, too, were a guarantee of security.

I also knew from an early age the contents of the upper drawers in my mother's bedroom opposite: lavender bags embroidered and enclosed with mauve or pink ribbon, many pairs of gloves in white or grey cotton, fur or leather, a number of purses, hand-bags and reticules, silk scarves, and, one drawer down, the brown fox fur that bit its own tail between its springed jaws. Later it became my habit, once my mother was safely downstairs, to make surreptitious raids among these feminine objects, in search of half-crowns, for my morning or evening visits to the Yeoman or the Compasses. My mother was perfectly aware of these regular raids. I even think she scattered a modest provision of half-crowns left fairly well in evidence, in order to prevent me from making too much of a mess among her neatly ranged piles of brightly coloured tiny patterned handkerchieves. But so long as I did not exaggerate –

taking a brown ten shilling note, for instance, my raids were never referred to. She knew that I knew that she knew. There was no need to say anything about it, and discretion saved us both from mutual embarrassment. It would have been awkward asking for or giving me such pocket-money when I was in my mid-thirties. But it was not just a matter of obtaining drink money. I was fascinated by the neatness with which my mother laid out and folded her blouses, and I liked rummaging among her hats, some of which had a pheasant's feather obtruding from the ribbon round the brim, others in blue straw, with floral arrangements. Here was a white parasol, with an ivory handle, and here a green silk one, with an ebony handle. I had not seen them in use for years; indeed I think they must have come from my grandmother's wardrobe in the Hythe. Some of the long, beaded reticules appeared to date from the pre-1914 period, so did a tiny gun-metal watch that hung on a long chain for evening wear. I enjoyed the *feel* of many of the silks and stuffs; but above all, like so many people and so many objects in Tunbridge Wells, the contents of the three top drawers – I was too discreet to push further down to the presumed domain of more intimate garments – of my mother's chest-of-drawers seemed to span the great divide between pre-War and post-War, as suited to a town in which the two periods continued to exist side-by-side, and without any apparent clash, throughout the twenties and indeed well on into the thirties.

It was the same with the heavy silver objects, all carrying, interlaced, the letters 'D.S.', the intitials of my mother's maiden name, on her dressing-table: a silver-backed hairbrush, a clothes-brush in black rosewood, with silver initials, a long silver button-hook that must have outlived its daily use by twenty or thirty years, a similar instrument, also silver, that may have had something to do with the immense complications of hooks-and-eyes, a silver container to an eau-de-cologne bottle. The dressing-table suggested a small museum to the enormous changes in feminine clothing brought by the events of 1914. They might have dated from my mother's twenties, at a period when she was about to leave for Bloemfontein, just after the Peace; or they might have been wedding presents dating from 1909; but this seemed unlikely, because, if they had been, they would hardly have been marked 'D.S.'. The huge leather hatbox that stood beside the bed was certainly pre-Boer War, or contemporaneous with that shameful event, hinting at a period when hats had been still vast and spreading and could only be transported in receptacles even vaster.

And so, going through my mother's upper drawers, or taking in, object by object, the contents of her dressing-table, and enumerating the formidable armoury of hat-pins, some of them coloured, some terminating in silver butterflies or insects, offered all the excitement of a small excursion through the history of female clothing over a period of forty or fifty years. It also revealed to me – laid out flat and well sprinkled with little white balls of camphor – the daily and weekly calendar of my mother's changes of clothing: silk for Bridge in the evening, a sober grey suit for Sunday service at King Charles, but also for weddings, light dresses for croquet at the Nevill Tennis Club, everyday tweeds or tussores – Tunbridge Wells was a very tussore place – for shopping, the yellow and brown beach coat for the seaside (or for sitting on the roof). I was amazed by the sheer extent of the possible metamorphoses; and while some of the dresses or suits or blouses were at once identifiable, as having been seen on the wearer on some particular occasion, or series of occasions, others struck an unfamiliar, even jarring, note, as if they did not go with my mother at all, or represented some aspect of her that had eluded me. As she grew older, she took increasingly to clearing out her old clothes, giving them to jumble sales, or, oddly, to the Church Missionary Society, a decision that I greatly regretted – though I was unable to express my regrets, for that would have been to reveal the extent and the thoroughness of my surreptitious investigations

– because it diminished the range of interest and the variety of the clothing archive. One thing my mother *never* threw out was shoes: there were armies of these, all low-heeled, all strong and sensible, brown, black, dark blue, beige, some with buckles, some with laces, as well as half-a-dozen pairs of tennis shoes (which would also come out at the seaside), and three pairs of Wellingtons, used for gardening (the gardening gloves were kept in a drawer in the dining-room). But the boots had gone, and there remained nothing to suggest that throughout her twenties and early-thirties my mother had ridden at least once, often twice, every day. The only reminder of that was a little silver-topped switch among the sticks in the hall. But the cupboard containing the shoes also housed eight tennis rackets and two badminton ones.

There was nothing improper about my investigations of the contents of my mother's drawers. They had started quite accidentally, as a result of routine searches for silver change; and they remained dictated purely by curiosity and by an enjoyment in the appearance and the feel and the sheen of pretty fabrics and soft silks and tussores. The objects fascinated me for two further reasons: because they were unfamiliar, and because their wearer was likewise unfamiliar. The relationship between my mother and myself was always reticent and entirely undemonstrative, governed by mutually recognised areas of silence and discretion. The nearest my mother ever got to displaying an emotion was to stand on the balcony, so that she could see the last of the taxi, as it turned into Grove Hill, each time I returned to Paris, after a stay in her house. As I took a last look at the erect, spare figure, I would think, with dread, that I might never see it again. But we never referred to such matters. I found the contents of her drawers moving, as well as interesting, because they seemed to speak of her. There was nothing more to it than that. I had never been inside my sister's bedroom, and I was 21 when she got married. And I was quite unfamiliar with – and extemely nervous of – girls until I was 24.

But I always liked the company of older women, and
Tunbridge Wells offered me a unique spectacle of two quite
distinctive periods of feminine clothing.

I never entered my father's small bedroom, and was away in
Paris when he died. After his death, my mother and my sister
had all his clothes burnt, as a no doubt unnecessary
precautionary measure, so that my only investigations in that
direction had been confined to the Colonial and Imperial
contents of the tin trunks in my father's room in the Hythe,
during his long absences in the Soudan. These bore no
relationship to the realities of his everyday Tunbridge Wells
wear: several oatmeal plus-four suits, all more or less identical,
though some more worn than others, long oatmeal stockings,
strong, very large brown shoes, and an oatmeal cap that,
perched on his head, accentuated the prominence of his large
sticking-out ears, and a pipe, also an article of clothing (pipes,
too, were burnt, perhaps suitably, if too late, for they had
certainly hastened, if not actually caused, his death). On
Sundays, a blue suit, and a light beige Homburg (which, at a
later stage, was to be the curse of my existence). So there had
never been any question of investigating in that quarter. Nor
would I have been tempted, had there been any possibility of it.
Having spent a number of years as a boarder, both at prep and
at public schools, I was only too familiar with the scattered,
dubious, and often pungent articles of masculine clothing, the
doubtful colours of pants, and with pyjamas that had got mixed
up and the lower halves of which had managed to change
partners. Like most people in that situation there was really
nothing that I did not know about the boy fully-clothed,
partially-clothed, or totally unclothed, about the Sunday boy
and the weekday boy, about the class-room boy and the
changing-room boy, about the Monday OTC boy (Monday,
therefore, with its dreaded military *smell*) and about the subtle
distinctions between boys' clothing and boys' privileges, or lack
of them. As with ladies, it was only the clothing of masculine

55

adults, even more, the elderly, that caught my attention and remained in my memory: my grandfather's narrow and many-buttoned jackets, old Dr Starling's morning-coat, striped trousers and top-hat, high-ranking clergymen in black leggings with wireless extensions to their hats, the panamas of the bowls players. In any case, masculine clothes were not pretty, they were not in soft, silky materials, they did not *feel* nice to the touch; only top-hats had that quality. It is true that, when I was 5 or 6, my mother dressed me in black velvet shorts, which she had made up on her Singer, and little white silk shirts. The penguin combination was no doubt appealing (as it always is, witness Eton College, or an Oxford Degree Day) but the inside of the velvet knickers gave me a red rash on the inside of my upper thighs, and the irritation persisted even after my mother had lined them with velveteen bands. I moved into my sister's bedroom when she got married, but it had been stripped of all traces of its previous occupant. The only surviving reminder of her former presence was a crest in a bright-red frame and a motto in some uncouth language which spelled out something like: 'Franc ha leal eto ge'; it might have been Glaswegian, or Anglo-Saxon; and I suppose my sister and her fellow-Godolphinians under the regime of CRASH – Miss C. R. Ash, the Headmistress, who lived to 99 – must have known what it meant. And there was a cricket bat in one of the cupboards (the girls at that school had had to play that horrible game). Neither object gave any hint of Baudelairean *douceurs féminities*.

7 THE BLACK WIDOW

So much for my mother's house (for I always thought of it as that, though my father had lived there, too; but he had hardly marked it with even a hint of his nine-year presence, perhaps he had never really been at home there, or indeed anywhere else out of Africa). The pictures on the walls were water-colours or oils by my mother, including one of St Leonard's House, the Hythe, as seen from the garden, or by her Ipswich teacher, the Suffolk painter, Barlow-Wood; the silhouettes were the work of my mother; the small sketches were by my sister's mother-in-law; the drawing of the skyline of Shrewsbury, as seen from the top of the Schools from the other side of the river, was my work; most of the books – with the exception of the Kiplings and the Conrads and *The Ingoldsby Legends*, my father's favourites – reflected my mother's reading tastes; the chair-covers were her choice; only the large, empty armchair and the pipe-rack hinted, rather timidly, at my father's former presence.

I have said that, in the Tunbridge Wells of the twenties and thirties, two different periods continued to exist, in apparent harmony, certainly not causing any particular surprise, side by side, as if the town had managed to retain one foot in the wonderfully secure and lavish world of Edwardian England, while the other stepped out, as vigorously as elsewhere, to the quick tunes of the twenties. Each warm summer of my early childhood would bring out the white silk, yellow or green parasols that had probably seen previous service in Baden-Baden, Karlsbad, or Homburg, the yellow tussore dresses of pre-war quality, and the alpaca coats and panamas of the elderly gentlemen who came and sunned themselves on the seats of the 'South of France'. The electric de Dion Bouton, apparently driven by two chauffeurs in bottle-green uniforms tight at the collar, though in fact there was only one, very evident, almost upright steering-wheel, still made its stately daily progress down Major York's Road, from Bishop's Down to Raiswell's Corner. The vehicle, the two chauffeurs, and its passenger, the lady in apparently changeless *toque* and silk dress in old rose, just as the old lady's heavily enamelled face seemed to have been set firmly in timeless immobility – actually survived into the Beveridge era. Dr Footner continued to visit his elderly patients in a carriage and four. Miss Amy Lake – the younger sister of Miss Lake, who spent her days reclining on a sofa, in a lavender dress and a lavender necklace that brought out the gentle blueness of her eyes – continued to wear the long black skirt, short Eton-style jacket, very tight at the waist, enormous, elaborately-flowered black straw hat, fur muff, sturdy black stockings and black buttoned boots that she had presumably acquired in the early nineteen-hundreds, her complicatedly piled-up black hair retaining its colour and its apparent abundance – as did her uneven black moustache – right into the forties. I think it was all her own hair and that the colour was natural, for Miss Amy was not a person to care in the least about appearance. Even the large man's umbrella that she always prudently carried, in all seasons, the moulting black fur round her neck, and the huge leather bag, attached to her arm, seemed changeless. She always shopped in the nearby Pantiles, accompanied by a little black, white and brown fox-terrier – she must have got through at least half-a-dozen during the period that I knew her – on a lead. Her shopping proceeded likewise in a changeless sequence, no doubt adopted in pre-War days. Dust's, for hat-pins and buttons, Durrant's, for dog-food, Porter's, for the replacement of rubber balls and other essential toys, Charlton's, for rhubarb and vegetables (the stalks of which, sticking from the huge bag, would indicate to the experienced observer the stage of shopping that had been reached, as well as the invariability of the Cumberland Walk menus), a pause at the bandstand, if the band were playing, though she would never sit down on one of the canvas chairs – indeed, I don't think I ever saw Miss Amy sitting down – and, finally, a visit to Jupp's, at the end of the Pantiles, where she replenished her stocks of a mild snuff and took on board the huge bag of further supplies of sweets for her pupils. I had known Miss Amy from the age of 5, when I had first gone to the establishment known as 'Miss Lake's', a strange-looking house entirely covered in round pebbles, up a steep, zig-zag path, high above Cumberland Walk, though I reached it from its less prestigious, unpebbled back. 'Miss Lake's' was an infant school, run by Miss Amy and her invalid elder sister, the foundation of which went back to a past so remote as to be unchartable. I have forgotten most of my contemporaries there, but can remember a son of Edgar Wallace, and a girl called Sheila Daley who had beautiful golden hair. I could see no significant change in Miss Amy, nor in her clothing and accompanying equipment, nor in the order of her shopping, nor in the briskness of her stride, thirty years later. Nor did she ever regard me other than as a five-year-old, though, in moments of indulgence, she might promote me to 8, the age at which I left the pebbled house, in floods of tears, to go to Rose Hill.

Any day, at any season, the Black Widow could be encountered on the Common, which seemed her natural habitat. Its dark, lowering rocks, covered in moss and fringes of stunted trees, seemed to have been contrived as a suitably dramatic background to this Gothic figure of bottomless Woe. Like the stunted trees, the Black Widow seemed to bend and falter in the face of the cruel wind and, even on days that were perfectly still, the immensely long black crêpe streamer that hung from her veiled head-dress and the wide sleeves of black material that gave her a winged appearance would flutter in crow-like dark movements, either ahead of her, obscuring her face and blinding her stumbling progress, or cracking straight out behind her, as if generating their own sources of wind-power. Her face, when glimpsed between the agile folds of black drapery, matched, indeed surpassed, the accompanying clothing, in sheer horror. It was terrifyingly thin, the eyes just dark sockets in a livid yellow skin. On one's first encounter, one would expect her to fall down dead at any moment, she appeared to carry the imminence of death in every part of her. She was almost too good to be true, as if she had been given a stage part as a professional *Veuve de Guerre*. I do not even know if she *were* actually a War Widow. My aunt, and other observers who had been in Tunbridge Wells before 1914, could recall her already tottering, windswept, across the more frequented macadam paths of the Common, during daylight, two or three years before the conflagration.

So the Black Widow was not *quite* what she appeared to be, and what she appeared to be was rather *too* much for Protestant, discreet Tunbridge Wells. There was an *excess* in the display of her grief, something Continental and Catholic. Furthermore, she did not merely haunt the Common; she could be seen, more rarely, on Mount Pleasant, as well as in Camden Road and even in Calverley Road, still accompanied by her retinue of personal winds. She had even been seen to enter shops, heard to order goods, in a voice that, far from sepulchral, was quite clear; she had even been heard to order *drink* – Bristol Cream, at Durrant's, in the Pantiles, to be delivered to an address in Warwick Park.

She continued to be a familiar figure, with all her drapes, and as changeless as Miss Amy, on the Common for all the years of my childhood. Even the children became accustomed to her, and no longer took fright at her sudden appearances from behind a clump of tall ferns or on a curve of the Old Race Course (the Common offered her plenty of suitable cover). My mother not only knew her name (which was, I think, Lady Napier), but had actually met her at Bridge; my mother added, with the authority of the green-baize table before her, that she was very nice.

The Black Widow, in short, seemed rather a let-down, as well as an object-lesson in not judging on first appearances. But she too, like the passenger of the electric car, Dr Footner, Dr Starling, Miss Amy, and even my aunt Emily, represented continuity. The Common would not have been the same without her. Over a long period she continued to appear to be on the point of death. I don't know when she actually *did* die; but it must have been when she was quite an old lady. She had become as much part of the familiar landscape as the Nevill

Bakery dwarfs, the one-eyed man in the book section of Goulden & Curry, and as the shabby, drooping, hopeless, listless, unshaven figure of despair in a filthy cap, an unlighted cigarette hanging from his lower lip, his dirty mac buttonless and flapping open, who sold (*sic*) the *Evening Argus* outside the Great Hall cinema, and on the wrong side of the Central Station. The last time I saw this familiar figure of despair, he seemed even more despairing than usual, as if about to topple over forwards; his unsold pile of papers was at his feet, he himself was holding a poorly printed poster, marked in red: 'German-Soviet Pact Signed'. I never saw him again after that dreadful day. Unlike the punctual and pretty predictable Black Widow, he disappeared from the scene. I enquired about him from several people, Kate included, from the bottom end of Grove Hill, as well as at the large and gloomy pub adjoining the Great Hall; but no one could enlighten me. It was almost as if I had been the only person in the whole town to have noticed him. I had often wondered why he looked so intensely wretched and beaten. Perhaps he was just terribly poor.

From my relatively low level – though it was very slowly getting higher – I went round with my eyes open and my ears (large, like my father's) attuned to every inflexion of adult speech, and, above all, quite blissfully unaware of my own proper enrolment in an age-group, whether of the under-tens, the under-twelves, or the under-sixteens. I travelled singly, not just as a matter of choice, but above all because there was hardly anyone of my own age to travel with, and, once I had become a boarder, Tunbridge Wells beckoned more insistently than ever as the longed-for place to be alone in. I certainly did not miss the companionship of those roughly of my own age; I hardly gave the matter a thought, any more than I was conscious of being 13 or 16. My current age did not seem to matter very much. I did not become a *promeneur solitaire* from any sort of romantic Rousseau-ite choice; it was merely that I was happy with my own company and with that, so rich and varied, of the topography of Tunbridge Wells and its neighbourhood, though, in my thirties and forties, I came more and more to appreciate the company of my mother and the shared enjoyment of our favourite stopping-places, as they were gradually reduced to a range more and more restricted: a sunny seat overlooking Crowborough Beacon, in Calverley Park; a seat on one of the bends of the Old Race Course, at a point where the ferns grew very high, competing with the tall mauve weeds, or just the view from the balcony of her drawing-room. Much of the later charm of Tunbridge Wells was that it was thus shared, representing an unspoken dialogue between the two of us.

My sense of apartness and the range of approaches to and from the town available to me were both enormously increased, and the former strengthened when, at 12, I was given a bicycle, from Halford's on Mount Pleasant, with all the most desirable accompaniments: a mirror, a horn, a speedometer, a milometer, a couple of deep saddle-bags that would take my sketching pad. Now I could take in the Medway Valley as far down as Wateringbury, as far up as Penshurst. Ruins covered in ivy, the remains of castles, fortifications and Bishops' Palaces, follies, towers, motes, meres, mill-ponds, the dry course of uncompleted canals, churches, windmills, sections of the Pilgrims' Way, dips in the North Downs, stretches of Ashdown Forest, the farther reaches of Eridge Park, the Bayham Estate, all these now opened up before me. Chiddingstone, Sissinghurst, Ightham, Wrotham, Hadlow, Mereworth, Mayfield, Rotherfield, Ticehurst, Ashurst, Flimwell, Lamberhurst, Goudhurst, Wadhurst, Hever invited me. I could get into the hop country beyond Paddock Wood; I could sketch a ruined palace near Otford, a clothes-line as seen from a village churchyard, the graves at all angles in the foreground, the shirts, pillow-cases, sheets, pyjamas, nappies, towels fluttering in the middle distance, on a windy day, a combination that had a particular appeal to me. Now I could find subjects for my sketch-book at every outing. I liked ruins best, as they gave the greatest opportunities for vigorous cross-hatching; but I equally favoured the bare winter trees and a winter landscape that blended with the possibilities of black-and-white. I was not quite such a newcomer to cycling as the adventurous and poetical Mr Hoopdriver; each of my excursions had to be confined, there and back, within a single day, and cycling was perhaps not quite so blissful in the early thirties as it had been in the pre-War days so eloquently described by H.G. Wells in *The Wheels of Chance*. But the country roads were still quiet and relatively free of traffic, the roads themselves, often between steep banks and high hedges, had human proportions; there were few lorries, and the green Maidstone & District buses were familiar and slow-moving. I only once set out with someone else – he had been imposed upon me – but I managed to shake him off on the way by suddenly turning down a side road. After that, I was left alone to plan my own outings, eating my sandwiches on a ridge, or on the banks of the Medway, or on the top of St John's Common, or in a churchyard, before settling on what to sketch. I covered a great deal of ground, only the coast and the estuaries remaining just out of reach; but I managed Bodiam. By the time I got back into the Tunbridge Wells area, I was generally so tired that I did not care *which* approach I took. I did not even mind coming in through Southborough, but my most gentle approach was via Pembury and the Pembury Road and down the top end of Grove Hill.

Tunbridge Wells now acquired both the prestige and the desirability of a *capital*. The capital of *what* I was not sure, probably of just about as far as I could cycle and back – but a capital all the same. I could see it as firmly set in the surrounding countryside, its vassal states that only acquired meaning and identity in virtue of their connection with the Wells (as the country people called it). I had in fact got it completely the wrong way round, for it was the surrounding countryside that owned and dominated much of the town, as the '*A*'s and the profusion of 'Camdens' would have informed me; and if Sir Henry Sidney and his brother appeared regularly at the Tunbridge Wells and Counties Club, the Nevills and the Pratts never graced the place, even if they did their shopping – or had it done for them – at Raiswell's. It is true that the country-side – particularly the bigger villages such as Brenchley, Paddock Wood, Lamberhurst, Goudhurst, and even farther afield: Tenterden, Marden – was largely dependent on 'the Wells' in one important respect: it supplied the principal outlet for daughters, drained away from the Medway Valley and the Weald as recruits to the still enormous army of domestic servants, not only in the big houses of Broadwater Down and the Parks, but in much humbler areas such as Grove Hill and Claremont Road. Among these migrants was Mrs Martin, who came to us as a 'daily' in 1926, and stayed until 1962. She was the seventh child – like my mother – of a hop-farmer from Horsmonden – her father, a patriarchal bearded man, once showed me round the inside of an oast-house. At 13 she had gone into service as scullery maid at a hotel on the Leas, in Folkestone, had moved to Tunbridge Wells in her late teens, working in a series of doctor's houses. My friend Wilfred Willett – who also sold the *Daily Worker* outside the Girls' Public High School and the Nevill Tennis Club (an *acte de présence* rather than a commercial undertaking) in the thirties – even managed to organise a trade union of female domestics, in the more favourable – because of the availability of war work – conditions of the forties, at a time when that particular rôle of the town was declining.

But I was not concerned with such niceties when I was at the peak of my cycling activities from 12 to 16. Each outing confirmed the importance of the place, and I felt it was a shame that the town could not announce itself from afar by a cluster of towers, spires, domes, castellations, fortifications, pinnacles, and even a cathedral or two; as it was, one generally came on the place quite undramatically, only the Crowborough Road offering the sudden view of the Wellington and Mount Ephraim, as if suspended in the sky.

If not a capital, Tunbridge Wells could certainly make claims to an identity that was unique and quite untypical of most places of its size. Its population structure was odd; while there was a heavy proportion of the over-sixties, native born Tunbridge Wellsians were relatively rare, at least among middle-class people, for quite a lot of the builders, tradesmen and shopkeepers were second or third generation (Weekes' celebrated its centenary in the sixties). Among the middle classes, most people had come from somewhere else; a few, like my father, from the Soudan; a great many more had come from India, a provenance recorded, perhaps rather unkindly, in the name given to a large and very handsome Regency house at the top of Mount Sion, which was always described locally as 'the Widows' Flats', though it did in fact have the more impressive and less revealing name of Cecil Court, written in gold letters above the classical portico. All the residents of the house (which had a superb garden and three tennis courts) were indeed widows of officers in the Indian Army, in the I.C.S. and in Indian Railways – what had happened to the husbands I do not know, though I tended to imagine that they had all been eaten by tigers. 'The Widows' Flats' provided a formidable intake to the Ladies' Bridge Club. Tunbridge Wells, if not at all Army & Navy, was to some extent Home & Colonial. The presence of this element among the middle-class population would no doubt have accounted for the rather surprising fact that the town offered no good boarding schools for boys, only two not very good prep schools, though girls were rather better provided for. Such people would have been in the habit of sending their male children away to be educated.

The owners of the big houses along Broadwater Down and the Pembury Road tended to be hard-faced northerners who, having made their pile in industry, had moved south and married middle-class girls from the south-east. Sammie Coad, the father of my school friend, Alan, had an unrepentant Leeds accent, was very direct, and rather liked shocking people; but Mrs Coad was almost excessively refined and moved about with silent grace, as if on invisible wheels, amidst a discreet rustle of silks and an aroma of discreet scents. At the beginning and end of each term, the Coads' chauffeur-driven brown Daimler, lined in beige, would call for me at Claremont Road, or deposit me there, on the trip to or from Crowborough. Alan and his mother (in light brown) occupied the back seat, so I would take a *strapontin*. It was a very smooth and comfortable journey, but I found the arrangement vaguely humiliating; my mother was always emphasising how 'careful' we had to be, but this seemed to be a case of getting something for nothing. My mother did not see it that way: 'it was very kind of Mrs Coad to have suggested the arrangement'. But I was fascinated by the interior of the car, and desperately wanted to use the speaking-tube, which had a little rubber horn covered over with beige crochet material. Mrs Coad used it two or three times on each journey to communicate with the straight back of the chauffeur in his brown uniform.

Mr Collins, the owner of Dunorlan, in the Pembury Road, was said to have made his money in shipping, either before or during the War. He was a Canadian, who had a lake in his garden. When the lake froze, as it appears to have done – at least in retrospect – every January or February, my father, wearing knickerbockers, would go and skate on it. It was an arrangement he had come to with Mr Collins. As I was not involved, I did not mind, in the way that I minded about the use of the Coads' Daimler.

8 DR RANKING

Perhaps the only *hereditary* element of the middle-class population was provided by the various dynasties of doctors. On my aunt's recommendation, we went first to Old Dr Starling, then to Young Dr Starling; then we switched to Old Dr Ranking, thence to Dr Ranking (his son), thence to Young Dr Ranking (his grandson). The three of them had been in practice for a total of eighty-five years. Young Dr Ranking, Jack, was a tiny little man – just over five foot – with everything: hands, feet, legs, arms, torso, head, in perfect proportion. He had been cox of the Cambridge boat – the rudder hung prominently in his consulting-room – and the fact that he was a 'blue' added to the prestige of what was already a prestigious practice. Jack drove a light grey Rolls with special attachments to the pedals to enable him to reach them. When he was driving, his small, very lined face – like that of a very knowing child who had seen a thing or two and who had had a good many worries – could be seen just above the level of the bonnet, his very dark hair neatly parted in the middle. He was the busiest doctor in this medical paradise. But, sometimes in the afternoons, he could be seen out walking, in a tiny sports-coat with eatable buttons and diminutive grey flannel trousers and suède shoes, by the Wellington Rocks, and exercising a dog that was almost as tall as himself, a vast spaniel who always seemed about to topple over his master. My mother swore by 'Little Jack' – not because of his medical skill, but because he was the son of his father ('a character') and the grandson of his grandfather ('a tartar'). He was the only person who had the slightest influence over her and who could get her to do things that she did not want to do. He bullied her into having a heater put in her Siberian bathroom, and even persuaded her not to have her bedroom window wide open in the February night. He even managed to get her to move for a spell to the Lansdowne and the Clarence Nursing Homes on three successive occasions. When he died suddenly, in his early forties – his heart packed in – she was deeply upset. No other doctor could replace 'Little Jack' and his quiet, but compelling authority. 'Now, Mrs Cobb, you will do as I say.' She had liked being bullied by the little chap. His death accelerated her mental decline.

The maid, who opened the door to his patients, at the vast grey house halfway up Frant Road, and whom he had inherited from his father and his grandfather, was called 'Whale'. This was apparently her real name, but she could have earned it from her quite amazing appearance as, fully rigged out as a senior maid of the nineties, an elaborate superstructure covering a network of whale-bone, cap with ribbons, white pinafore in stunningly white lace, an armour of stiff white frontage, black silk dress, black stockings and buckle-shoes, she opened the front-door with what appeared to be a sort of curtsey and with a smile that, though toothless, managed to remain welcoming. Whale was just under six foot, though very bent under the years of family service. Some of Little Jack's prestige was accountable to Whale's vintage antique appearance, perfect down to the last detail. Seeing Whale was part of the attraction of a consultation. In Tunbridge Wells, ancient retainers were held in high esteem and genuine affection, their devotion reflecting on the consideration in which their employers were held. For a doctor, Whale was a godsend; she seemed – and was (no one knew by how many years) immensely antique, and at the same time changeless; she had an incredible memory for names and faces, her manner was deferential, but firm, and, for people who were not feeling very well, or who were worried about their heart or their kidneys, she presented a figure of total indestructibility, almost a local monument. Indeed, it was impossible to conceive of a Tunbridge Wells without Whale. People used to talk about her and her memorable appearance. What became of her after her master died and the big house was sold, I cannot bear to think, but I do know that she was well provided for. She was held to be the *doyenne* of the domestic servants, though I think some of the butlers and coachmen must have been in harness almost as long. Jack Ranking – though married (to a very beautiful young woman, who was of normal size, like his father, his grandfather, his brother and his sister) – had no children; and the medical line ended with him. His brother was a barrister.

I missed him almost as much as my mother did. For, like so many family doctors – including my uncles Jack and Vernon, my mother's brothers – he was a very acute observer and a marvellous gossip. It was from him that I learnt some of the more surprising secrets regarding the seamier side of life in the Royal Borough and its neighbourhood: naughty parties in houseboats on the Medway (a river of sin), faces slapped and even fisticuffs in public, cheating at cards, middle-class girls who had disappeared to London for a month or six weeks, returning looking rather pale, clergymen in trouble over choirboys, the aftermaths of Hunt Balls in the Pump Room, the rather *risqué* parties given by the French master at Skinners' School, the furtive adventures of an antique-dealer who kept fairly open house in his rooms over the closed walk of the Pantiles (the location made these adventures sound even more wicked), some of the nastier tricks of the young City bloods, how the son of a local dentist had managed to get out of the War on somewhat spurious medical grounds, family disputes over wills, or the largely imaginary maladies of well-to-do old ladies for whom the weekly visit from their doctor represented a social event to be looked forward to. He told me that his best patients were those with nothing the matter with them. All such foibles he regarded with amused indulgence, taking them all in from a very philosophical height in marked contrast to his own. When standing at full height, he could just about see over the level of my mother's bed. With patients in old-fashioned high beds, he had to stand on a stepped stool, which he carried along with him in the Rolls, together with his black doctor's bag. One soon forgot about his height; Jack Ranking was universally liked and, as a doctor, he was enormously respected and much sought after.

I never heard of any *new* doctor coming to Tunbridge Wells and 'putting up his plate'; it would have been a very unwise thing to have attempted. Dr Davies (*Eyes*) and Dr Wood (*Ear & Throat*), who were consultants at my aunt's hospital, had inherited their practices – and their large houses – from their fathers. Dr Grace had merely moved in from a nearby village where his father had been a G.P. Even my school-friend at Rose Hill, Lemerle, who later had a Panel practice among the inhabitants of Calverley Road and of the areas behind St James's church (Mrs Martin, who lived in a little neat half-house in Cromwell Road, a poky little street – the Lord Protector could not have expected anything better in a town the original parish of which was that of King Charles the Martyr – was one of his patients), had succeeded his father. For a mere *Panel* doctor, he was said to have been both experienced and considerate. There had to be one or two 'on the Panel', even in a place like Tunbridge Wells.

If, then, few doctors moved to Tunbridge Wells, a great many people moved to Tunbridge Wells for the doctors, though, for a decade or so in the late forties and early fifties, there was a counter-movement in the direction of Eastbourne, a number of my mother's elderly female friends transferring themselves to the seaside and their custom to Dr John Bodkin Adams, whose fame and delightful bedside manner had spread inland as far as the Royal Borough. Most of these – when they survived – remained faithful to the seaside doctor even after his trial. It was fortunate that my mother had young Dr Ranking, otherwise she too might have been tempted to transfer, so much praise had she heard over the Bridge tables on the subject of the Eastbourne Wonder. Not possessing a Rolls, nor even an ordinary car, nor any external sign of unusual affluence, she would probably have been in safe enough hands with him, though his fees were said to be unusually steep, even by Tunbridge Wells standards.

There were also dynasties of homoeopaths, and matching homoeopathic patients – it seemed to have something to do with being a Quaker, though the connection may have been quite fortuitous – but I did not know much about either. My mother (the daughter of a Victorian country G.P.) regarded homoeopaths as 'not proper doctors', no doubt in virtue of that extra-stringent medical orthodoxy so often affected by female members of medical families who did not themselves practise medicine. (According to my mother, only people trained at Bart's were any good, her brothers had been there, though she would make a rather reluctant allowance for Guy's; St Thomas's was, apparently, 'no good'. Bart's hovered over the whole of my childhood, like a sort of awesome and much-invoked medical Holy Ghost: the awesomeness emphasised by the drop in my mother's voice when pronouncing the sacred monosyllable, though, for years, I had no idea what it stood for, perhaps some prestigious Dr Bart?) Such was the hold of conventional medicine over my mother's judgments and sense of proper hierarchies that, when far advanced in senile dementia, she would only communicate with my friend and former colleague, Richard Spilsbury. Anyone with *that* surname *must* be all right, and from the moment that she had first met him, she had spotted the relationship to the famed Sir Bernard.

9 KING CHARLES THE MARTYR

In my copy of *A Child's Life of Jesus*, the principal subject of the biography had longish sandy hair, parted down the middle, like the cashier in the Pantiles branch of Barclay's Bank, and he wore a striped robe rather like the seat of a deck-chair – and black sandals. The disciples were similarly clothed and had fair or reddish hair brushed away from the face. Only Judas was dark, with rather greasy black hair, so, having had *Westward Ho!* read to me in the evenings, in the house in Cumberland Gardens, I thought he must be Spanish, or perhaps a gypsy. Indeed, Jesus and the disciples not only had fair hair, they had middle-class faces, which made their clothes all the odder. Mary Magdalene had *red* hair; my mother said she looked very *Irish*, so, clearly she did not belong at Christ Church, nor at King Charles, nor at Holy Trinity, nor at St John's, nor at St James's, nor at the grand church for millionaire Christians in Broadwater Down, in monkey-puzzle-tree territory; *her* place would have been at the foreign-looking Catholic Church up beyond the Five Ways, and facing onto the entrance to the already alarming Upper Grosvenor Road, where the rough people lived. I used to walk past the Catholic Church in some trepidation, wondering what went on in there; once or twice I passed it when the doors were wide open, and it seemed very dark inside; there was a little red light at the far end, there was a funny smell, too. When we were living in Cumberland Gardens, we faced onto the back of the big, rather elegant neo-classical Baptist chapel, which gave its name to Chapel Place; we could see the people coming out on Sunday evenings; they seemed dressed normally, and my mother said that they were certainly respectable people: tradesmen, shopkeepers, and that sort of thing. Later, after we had moved to Claremont Road, I used to pass a small chapel that looked like a cinema, at the bottom of Grove Hill. I was very curious about this place, which had a corrugated-iron roof, and from which would come the sound of very cheerful singing, to the accompaniment of a piano. These were Pentecostals; my mother thought that they probably came from behind the Town Hall. They seemed very friendly when they came out in the road, standing about on the brick pavement talking to a big red-faced man with his dark hair brushed down, dressed in a blue suit, and who shook everyone very vigorously by the hand; *he* had very big red ones. I felt rather drawn to the place. But I never dared push open one of the green-baize doors and go in; it was just that I was frightened about crossing into a different social level, not knowing what such people would make of me, they might think that I was prying.

Of course, my sister and I did not need to be reminded of the dangers of Christian Science. We both had vivid and terrifying memories of something that had happened in Frinton days, and that my sister had told me about, in whispers, when I was 3. Two children, a boy of 7 and a girl of 11, had gone to a Christmas Party in Fourth Avenue dressed as the Snow King and the Snow Queen, covered, from head to foot, in cotton wool; they had come too close to the candles on the Christmas tree and had gone up in a sheet of flame, rushing out like torches, and rolling in the thick snow. As their parents were Christian Scientists, they would not call the doctor (old Dr Trench, who had delivered me, also in Fourth Avenue, but further up) and only prayed; after a week of awful suffering, both children had died. Much later, when I was 9 or 10, a girl who had been at Miss Lake's with me, and who lived half-way down Madeira Park, developed appendicitis; *her* parents, too, were Christian Scientists, so, of course, the poor child had died. There must have been quite a lot of devotees of that cruel faith, for there was an enormous circular church with a dome and that looked like an ice-rink, half-way between Tunbridge Wells and Southborough. There was also a reading room by York House in the High Street. I took care not to read anything that was displayed in the window.

Just below my aunt's hospital, as you went down the steep slope of Mount Sion, one could not help noticing a modest-looking little chapel with the intriguing title of 'the Countess of Huntingdon's Connection'. I was impressed, it seemed the right sort of Connection to be in; but it must have been very

select, for, in all my childhood, I never saw anyone go in or
come out. In the course of my excursions in search of
semi-ruined gardens, I had also spotted a large Methodist
church, off Mount Ephraim, next-door to the new hospital; the
church had been built many years before the Kent & Sussex;
even so, it seemed a good location, and it did occur to me, one
day when I saw there was a hearse standing outside, that it must
have done quite a brisk trade in the dead. Unfortunately,
having left Rose Hill by then, I had got out of touch with my
friend Hickmott, who later went into his father's firm.

Was there a synagogue in Tunbridge Wells? Certainly, I
never heard of one. For that matter, I hardly every heard of any
Jews. There was old Mrs Phillips, a Bridge friend of my
mother's, who was very rich – Black Cat cigarettes – and who
lived in Broad water Down; and there was her son, Artie, who,
so my sister tells me, was debagged and left standing only in his
pants, by the young City bloods of the 5.50 from Cannon
Street, some time in the early thirties; after that, he had driven
to London and back every day in his open green Bentley; he
used to overtake my sister's Baby Austin each morning,
between Hildenborough and Sevenoaks, when she was *driving*
to her teaching job at Westerham. But I knew nothing of this at
the time; the horrible incident would have seemed to have
belonged, by rights, to the late twenties, a case of that decade
flowing into the staider, more questioning, more liberal
thirties. Were there Jewish boys at Rose Hill, the Beacon, at
Shrewsbury? Perhaps there were; but I have no idea. At
Shrewsbury, in my House, there were some Liverpool
Unitarians, and very nasty bullies they were too. I hardly heard
Jews even referred to, save in respect of Mrs Phillips, whom
my mother liked – she was a very good Bridge player – and
whose generosity in setting aside a large house overlooking the
Happy Valley for refugee children she admired. Mrs Phillips,
she said, was a good and charitable woman. I only *read* about
Jews, and about anti-semitism, in *The Brown Book of the Nazi*

Terror, which was stocked in the window of Goulden & Curry, beside an illustrated biography in colour of Princess Marina, and several books on Kentish gardens, in 1935. Of course, there may also have been Jews who did not advertise themselves as such. What was quite clear to me at the time – and I accepted my mother's judgments in most social matters – was that there was nothing wrong with being Jewish (especially if one lived in Broadwater Down); it was not like being a Catholic (why, I wondered, often with bitter regret, at least at my two prep schools, had my parents inflicted on me the unspeakable initials of R.C.C?).

My mother went to King Charles because, she said, the vicar (Canon Oliver) was a gentleman, and because his sermons were sensible and short. King Charles, despite its name, was Low. Most of her Bridge, tennis and croquet friends went there, hatted and gloved, and, in the winter, wearing furs of different colours with little yellow eyes and a tiny spring device that enabled them to bite their own tails. She never went to communion; I think she regarded it as popish, at least flamboyant – only matins. She had a prayer-book in rich brown leather, her sister had one in a binding of silver decorated with the heads of cherubs. Her dog-headed umbrella – a yellow beast, showing its teeth, and made of china – would also be part of the Sunday equipment, alternating with a white silk sunshade with an ivory handle, for use in summer. She sat, as always, bolt upright – she even *knelt* upright – looking neither to the right nor to the left, though, after the service, she could identify everyone who had been present and in which pew and on what side of the aisle they had been sitting. My aunt, in virtue of longer residence, had a pew several rows further up. There would be a halt outside the main entrance after the service. It was the only day of the week on which the various female couples would be unaccompanied by their dog-attendants, giving each couple an oddly uncompleted appearance, though compensated for in part by the replacement of sensible flannel, worsted, tweed, and jaeger by shimmering silks and fabrics. The men – a minority – stood apart, looking rather lost and trying not to appear impatient to get away. The gentleman-vicar, wearing his white Cambridge hood – a point very much in his favour with my mother – would have a word with all the ladies, starting off with those living on Frant Road, Mount Sion next; Claremont Road came rather low down in the order of presentation. It was not in his parish, in any case. If not my mother – then my aunt – would have noticed – and commented on – the presence or the absence in the congregation of a very gracious figure in black silk and pearls and an enormous hat with osprey feathers, and carrying an embroidered reticule, a former Lady-in-Waiting to Queen Mary, and the cause of the latter's frequent, and, by the antique-dealers of the Pantiles – much dreaded – visits to the Royal Borough.

For most of my father's lifetime, we abandoned King Charles (I don't think my father liked gentlemen-vicars) and, every Sunday, walked the three miles to Speldhurst, getting back to a late lunch, myself very tired after the three miles back. I don't know why it had to be Speldhurst, though the walk there was very pretty, taking us, at one stage, within sight of the shack in which lived one of the local hermits; it had a long metal pipe as a chimney, sometimes with thick yellow smoke coming out. This hermit was never actually seen. Speldhurst church was unremarkable; the west window had ugly Victorian glass, and the parishioners seemed smart and well-to-do, in contrast to our own either dusty, muddy or sodden appearance. The vicar, Canon Masters, was a hearty, muscular Christian, given to sporting or schoolboy metaphors in his sermons. My father, who, as a young man in Peterborough, before he had volunteered for the Boer War, had rowed on the Nene in an eight which included a curate, greatly admired the Canon, a real *man*, he said, a point that I did not dispute; but I had a deep loathing for him; he seemed to be an ecclesiastical bully. I don't know what my mother thought of him; but he did not wear a Cambridge hood. So, Sunday after Sunday, in all seasons, we made the six-mile journey, through footpaths, over stiles, into fields with bulls in them, in order to hear Canon Masters. I do not know what he made of the four of us: my mother, her normally ruddy face purple or mauve, according to the season, and dressed in stout weekday shoes and country clothes, my sister carrying with her, there and back, one of her eloquently prolonged sulks, myself looking either hot and dusty, or like a drowned rat, my father aggressively jokey and in his most appalling Gilbert & Sullivan mood, especially if the weather had been unusually foul. He clearly saw in the Canon one whom he took to be a kindred spirit; but I am not sure that the feeling was reciprocated. The vicar had some very wealthy parishioners, and, behind the man-to-man language, there lay a good deal of worldliness. And, of course, we were *not* parishioners, just walking (and pretty dishevelled) hangers-on, camp-followers from the town, just as, during the week, we might so often be camp-followers at the meets of the Eridge Hunt.

My father, on retirement from the Soudan, had thought of Tunbridge Wells only as a temporary stopping-place, a halt that would give him time to find something permanent in the country. Almost up to his death, he kept up the plan for an eventual move to a Kentish or a Sussex village. Kent and Sussex in the twenties and thirties were not what they are now; there were still genuine villages – though Speldhurst was not one – inhabited by labourers and rural craftsmen. I think the Sunday walks to Speldhurst must have been part of this, in fact illusory, preoccupation with a rural retreat; regular attendance at a rural church might have seemed to be giving him literally a foot in the parish, a sort of moral presence, soon to be materialised into a physical one. As he was a tireless walker, whether exercising other peoples' dalmatians, or alone, he had covered every footpath, minor road and track within a twelve-mile radius of Tunbridge Wells, knew every dog and every farmer in the neighbourhood, and must have noted down a score or more of possible choices. Canon Masters may have had quite a lot to do with the Sunday choice of Speldhurst, but there must have been more to it than that: more even than my father's natural inclination to combine simple and energetic piety with simple and energetic forms of exercise. I really do not know just what he had in mind when he imposed on the three of us these weekly Pilgrimages of Grace over waterlogged fields and through muddy lanes. Perhaps he was thinking in pictorial terms of one of those mid-Victorian coloured prints, a naive nineteenth-century map of Pilgrim's Progress to Salvation, up steep, narrow, craggy paths, with roaring lions and fierce, foaming beasts waiting at every turn, and temptresses beckoning from the long grass and lush comfort of every inviting meadow. The more difficult the way, the greater the reward. Whatever it may have been, it was certainly an illusion, one of his rare and cherished fantasies; for nothing would in fact have induced my mother to leave Tunbridge Wells, her Bridge, tennis and croquet partners, and her sister Emily. Of course, as always, she had the last word. After my father's death, in 1935, she returned, I think with relief, to the less strenuous King Charles. It was a sensible sort of church for a sensible sort of parishioner. Speldhurst had been one of my father's more bizarre enthusiasms. We never returned there after his death. My mother could feel as much at home in King Charles as in the Ladies' Bridge Club or the Nevill Tennis Club; indeed, King Charles was just the Sunday version of the two latter, the only difference being that the social function took place in the morning, whereas Bridge, tennis and croquet were only in the afternoon or evening. It was also an opportunity to wear the fox fur with the yellow eyes, to carry her best leather bag and the leather-bound prayer-book. My mother's family had a relaxed and sensible attitude to established religion as a desirable social function, and they no doubt felt that my father displayed a rather unseemly enthusiasm. My aunt Emily went to King

Charles, because the doctors went there; my uncle Jack went to the big Victorian church in Theale, because his wealthier patients went there; my uncle Percy went to the garrison church in Portsmouth, because he was a surgeon-commander in the Navy and it was part of the drill; my aunt Mabel went to the parish church at Chevening because the Earl of Stanhope went there; my aunt Jane went to Girton chapel because she was Garden Steward of the college, my uncle Vernon went to the Greek Orthodox Cathedral in London because his wife was Greek and Orthodox. Only my aunt Mary, a loner and the most independent member of my mother's family, and also the kindest, the gentlest, the most generous, and the most unassuming, a tiny little woman, birdlike, with sharp grey eyes behind a pair of rimless pince-nez – *never* went to church; and, after I had left school, she was in the habit of asking me to sherry, at her flat in St John's Wood, followed by lunch, with wine, in a restaurant nearby; sherry was always at eleven sharp, so as to exclude church. But then she lived alone, and in London, and did not have to worry about what other people thought. Later, she died alone, in her flat; and her body was not found for three days. No one had noticed. She would have liked such an unobtrusive exit.

10 THE OUTSIDE WORLD

I have little memory of *politics*. It does not seem to have been a political town. I had noticed the local headquarters of the Conservative Party, not because of that, but because Thackeray had lived in it while writing *The Newcomes*, giving the house, which faced onto the Common, a great deal of prestige in my eyes. If I *had* known anything about politics, I might have asked myself why the Conservative Party should have *needed* a headquarters in Tunbridge Wells. The M.P., Colonel Spender-Clay (a name that seemed to spell out affluence), if not hereditary, was perpetual, though I believe he did eventually have a successor at the end of the thirties. After the War the constituency was represented by the son of Mrs Wellington-Williams, a lady who played Bridge and lived in an enormous house on Frant Green, so perhaps being double-barrelled was a condition of acceptance.

I believe my parents regarded themselves as Liberals; at least, they read a Liberal newspaper for as long as it lasted; both professed concern for the Underdog (a concern I did not share, *any* sort of dog filling me with apprehension and loathing).

During the General Strike, my father had been sworn in as a Special Constable and had been provided with a blue-and-white striped armband and a wooden truncheon with a leather thong (which he was allowed to keep, for I still have it); but I don't think he ever had to use it. Certainly, Whale and her colleagues below-stairs never went on strike. Apparently some of the trains were driven, it was said, by 'undergrads'. Cook was a distant, malignant figure, who lived very faraway, somewhere in the north. The same year I do remember reading, on the front page of the *Westminster Gazette*, of the death of the King of Roumania, who had a beard; there was a photograph of him surrounded by a black border, so he must have been an ally. I don't remember any political news in the weekly *Children's Newspaper*; and there certainly wasn't any in the *Modern Boy*. My mother and I once went to stay in a large and very magnificent hotel at St Leonards. In the drawing-room, there was a wireless and, during the 6 o'clock news, there were many references to an Anglo-Japanese Naval Conference.

When I was 13, there was much talk in the house about 'going off the Gold Standard'. This was apparently a very dreadful thing to have happened, but it did not have any visible effects on Tunbridge Wells; no building fell down, there were no reports of sudden deaths, or of people throwing themselves out of windows, the event was not referred to in Sunday sermons, the shops – and, worse, the schools – remained open.

The outside world

We never had a wireless before the outbreak of the War. But each Christmas Day, from some time in the early thirties, I was invited to the flat next door, the home of the widow of a bank manager, Mrs Stephens – my mother and I always referred to her as 'Stebbins', which seemed to suit her fussiness about minor proprieties – who looked like a be-ribboned sheep and dressed in light rose, to match the chair-covers and heavy velvet curtains of her over-furnished and over-heated drawing-room. Her appearance would be more sheeplike than ever on this particular day, following a visit to the hairdresser on Christmas Eve, her white hair set in several series of neat-looking curls. The room would be quite stifling, with an enormous fire blazing in the grate. As this was a very solemn annual occasion, I was given a glass of very sweet sherry. We would listen, standing up and facing the blazing fire (I could not help thinking that it would have been more suitable if we had faced the wireless, which was where the Voice came from), to the King's Christmas Message. We would remain standing for the National Anthem, after which we sat down on two French-style chairs. After finishing my sherry, I would take my leave, thanking Mrs Stephens for her annual hospitality, and puzzling over why we always had to face the fire. The likeliest explanation seemed to be that it was in the general direction of Sandringham or wherever the Voice was speaking from.

On a dreadful day in September 1939 – a particularly luminous early-September day – my mother and I were sitting in deckchairs on the flat roof. It might have been ten or thereabouts, when Mrs Martin came up (she had a wireless in Cromwell Road), saying: 'The Germans are at them Poles, Ma'am'. I felt as if I had swallowed a huge lump of ice. The Wellington, the Earl's Court, the Regency houses of the top-dentists and the tower of Rusthall church and the rest of Mount Ephraim all remained in place, everything *looked* just the same; but nothing could *ever* be the same. Politics were getting too close to Tunbridge Wells. Mrs Martin had an only child, a very quiet, well-spoken boy called Gordon, then about 13 and doing well at school. Sometimes he came with his mother in the morning and would play silently with my old toys. When he was just over 18, he went over to Normandy with the West Kents, after little more than six weeks' initial training, and was killed almost immediately. Mrs Martin did not blame the Germans, she blamed Churchill, for whom she conceived, though a peaceable person, a keen supporter of the Salvation Army and a regular Sunday attendant at the Battery, quite near her home, an undying and uncharacteristic hatred. She claimed that he had *enjoyed* every minute of a War that had deprived her of her only child, an innocent, scarcely out of his boyhood. For years afterwards, while taking their 'elevenses', my mother in the dining-room, Mrs Martin in the kitchen (*nothing* would have induced her to sit down in the dining-room), the door kept open between them to facilitate communication, they would talk about these things: poor Gordon, and the cruel Churchill. My mother thought Mrs Martin was quite right; *any* mother, she asserted, would have felt the same.

They did, however, have *other* subjects of conversation: one, apparently inexhaustible, concerned Mrs Martin's perpetual lodger (a competitor, in duration, to our M.P.), a young man – or he had been young when he had first come to lodge in Cromwell Road – who worked in the Post Office, and who, with good prospects of promotion, had been engaged to the same girl for over ten years – he had even built a bungalow in Matfield for the matrimonial home, and would go there regularly at week-ends to add to it. But there was always some reason for the wedding to be put off, and the lodger was still with her in his forties. Mrs Martin darned his socks, did his washing, and gave him his breakfast and his supper, all of which may have had something to do with his prudent reluctance to change status. I enjoyed this subject, for it suggested continuity rather than change. The lodger had been hesitating on the brink in the thirties, the brinkmanship was carried through the War years, and he was still hesitating – rather more theoretically – in the early fifties. I believe he *did* go to the bungalow, now a bungalow no longer, for it had acquired an upper storey, magnificently appointed, and fully stocked, as if for a siege or for a family of eight – in the end, but alone.

Such then was the speed at which politics had accelerated in Tunbridge Wells between September 1939 and June 1944. It was not a safe place any more. It even became a military headquarters: a presence visible, every week-day, at 7.30 in the morning, from my mother's bedroom, in the shape of little strings of obese, red-faced figures, in running-shorts and vests, in scattered groups of dejected twos and threes, puffing along Claremont Road. General Montgomery was in town, sending even his Staff officers on their daily early morning run. Fitness was the thing, but they did not *look* the least bit fit, as they toiled, gasping, in the direction of the stone crocodiles. Old Mr Weekes, who could be sighted every morning on the stroke of 7.20 carrying his bathing dress and towel on his way to the public baths, now had (rather unwilling) competitors, in the cult of regular physical exercise. The town had been invaded, its privacy had been breached, it had started slowly going downhill as the officers slowly ran uphill. Lilac front doors with carriage-lights beside them and hanging white baskets of flowers and foliage over them would be next.

But the decline was not immediate, being spread, in patches, over a long period of years. If Broadwater Down had been definitively breached, the gated Parks had struggled on, relatively inviolate. There were still plenty of *safe* houses, protected by thick privet hedges and friezes of yews and monkey-puzzle trees, along Lansdowne Road, or up towards St John's; and if the younger female servants simply disappeared, the older ones – the Whales and their kind – remained answering the door with changeless solemnity, and still managing to obtain starch for their stiff white head-dresses and armoured linen fronts.

11 THE LIMBURY-BUSES

One of the most reassuring pockets of resistance to change was provided by my maternal cousins, the Limbury-Buses, a family consisting, in 1939, of old Mr and Mrs Limbury-Buse, in their mid-seventies, their son, Geoff, well on in his forties, and their daughter, Olive, in her early forties, and a well-starched maid in her seventies. The Limbury-Buses lived in a big Victorian house named Florian with a dank, dripping, overgrown garden, near a large gothic pinnacle in stone erected to the memory of Canon Edward Hoare, a noted nineteenth-century preacher and vicar of Holy Trinity Church, whose features in profile adorned one side of the monument. The house was on the road to Southborough and quite close to St John's church (which my cousins were never able to attend, owing to difficulties of time-table). They had occupied the house since the nineties. Though *aware* of the War – not that they ever read any newspapers, or listened to the wireless (the only one was in the kitchen), they made absolutely no concessions to it, maintaining the daily routines that had been gradually established over the previous twenty or thirty years, and that, by the time I came on the scene, had been frozen into a slow-moving ritual, prudent and solemn (Geoff and his father moved forward as if they had been royal heralds walking backwards, unhurried and stately) and fixed for ever. Old Mr Limbury-Buse had read Law at Cambridge with a view to 'taking articles' and practising as a solicitor. But, as he had been of delicate health, his parents had decided that he should not work, and he had moved to Tunbridge Wells in order to have a quiet time. In this, he had been entirely successful. He had never done a day's work since leaving Cambridge. Nor had he even been known to read, since that distant spurt of intellectual activity, unless the ability to distinguish between hearts, spades, diamonds and clubs, between ace, king, queen and jack, can be described as reading.

84

His son, Geoff, had followed his example, though he had failed to improve on it, having, after leaving Tonbridge, been caught up in the First World War, serving throughout it as an officer, and having then for a few years been involved in the film industry in Hollywood, though I do not know in what capacity. This spurt of energy had not been maintained; he had decided to stay at home, in the big house, so as to be near his parents. There had been no *need* for him to go on working, in any case, as the family enjoyed a steady income. Olive, however, did work, for a part of each year at least. In peacetime, she spent each autumn and winter in Switzerland, as an instructress in Winter Sports to English visitors. This period of activity was brought to an end, however, in September 1939, when she, too, settled down, apparently quite happily, to the slow tempo of Limbury-Buse family life.

Geoff, Olive and their parents had breakfast brought up in trays to their bedrooms at 9 o'clock. They were copious breakfasts, and remained so throughout the War. Geoff got up at midday. The old people and Olive had their lunches brought up in trays. Geoff had his alone, downstairs, handing down bits to a very old black dog who awoke briefly from his sleeping place under the table. Mrs Limbury-Buse got up at 3, in order to prepare for tea, a very splendid meal, involving a great deal of silver, and a variety of little trays, which I would attend once or twice a week. The quality and range of the Limbury-Buse teas gave no hint of wartime austerity, making them doubly attractive to me. There was something particularly agreeable in thus turning one's back on the world conflict, while working one's way through cucumber sandwiches, cream buns, chocolate cake, and cake with jam filling. I always dressed in civilian clothes, on these visits; khaki would have been obtrusive.

Geoff went out every day at 2, carrying a shopping-bag, and dressed, like my father, in an oatmeal jacket and plus-fours. His route was invariable: past the Kent & Sussex Hospital, then along the edge of the Common, past Thackeray's house, a purchase at Romary's biscuit shop, thence to the Tunbridge Wells and Counties Club. As he moved with majestic slowness, he would not reach the club till 2.30. After playing a rubber or two of Bridge, he would have tea at the club, then a single sherry; home by the same route, for 6.30.

His father left the house at 3.30 after dressing with great care and deliberation between 2 and 3. He did not take Geoff's route, going down to the Five Ways, then down Mount Pleasant and Vale Road, rounding the Post Office, to reach the club, on the stroke of 4, in time for tea. He and Geoff sat at different tables, never played together, and never spoke to one another while at the club. The old man left the club at 6.30, to reach home, by the route on which he had come, by 7.

Supper was at 7.30 and was the only meal attended by the Limbury-Buse family. Everyone went to bed at 9. On Sundays, Geoff too had lunch in bed, but got up for a walk along Mount Ephraim, as far as the Wellington, dressed in a blue suit. He was back for tea, attended by his sister and parents, who had just dressed. Drinks at home at 6.30. Cold supper at 7.15. Bed, as other days, at 9.

Geoff was generally silent, his only sign of sociability being a slow, gentle smile and a shake of the head. Mrs Limbury-Buse was very talkative, coming out with such items of information as that she had not been to the ladies' Bridge club for twenty-five years, had not been as far the Pantiles for fifteen, and had not taken a train since the age of 22. How nice it would be, she said, to see more of dear Dora (my mother, and her cousin), but it was much too far and Grove Hill was so steep; could not I persuade my mother to climb the hill and come and see them for tea, she was such a good walker, had always been? Olive would rattle away during tea about Switzerland, and the people that she had known there. I noticed that she was getting rather untidy and a bit neglectful of her appearance. She liked talking about Switzerland, but I did not have the impression that she missed the place. I think she was quite content to be

86

back with her quiet, affable, smiling brother, her talkative mother, and her rather vacant father. I could understand why, for each was entirely predictable, and there was a changelessness about their whole manner of life that excluded quite successfully such external horrors as wars, civil disturbances, class conflict, or, indeed, anything unfamiliar.

I never appreciated the Limbury-Buses and their sheltered, heavily-curtained routine so much as during the War years and those that followed. I knew, to the precise point, at what stage Geoff and his father would be, at any given time, on their separate afternoon progresses. And this being so, there was still somewhere safe, whatever was happening elsewhere. And, once back in town, I could check up on their movements for myself. They were as reliable as the many clocks in their dark, heavily furnished drawing-room. I needed to know that the Limbury-Buses were still on course; they represented, well on into my thirties, a solid link with my childhood and with a Tunbridge Wells that I wanted to be changeless, while knowing that it couldn't be. The house offered me an occasional haven; but for them it really was a haven. My attitude to Tunbridge Wells itself, once I had emerged from childhood, was ambivalent; I needed the place as somewhere to retreat to when things got rough; I needed to know that it was still there and ready to receive me back.

There was something splendid in their dismissive attitude towards the War, just a minor inconvenience that kept Olive from her seasonal work; and Olive had settled back easily enough into the family mould of organised idleness. Of course, Geoff and his father must have known that bombs had fallen on the town. But I am quite sure that, back in the dark, cluttered house, they would never have breathed a word of it to the old lady, to Olive and the ancient maid.

Old Mr Limbury-Buse and. Geoff also compelled my admiration for their total lack of *ambition*, as if they had never known the meaning of the word, or had long since forgotten it.

In this sense, too, they lived outside the conventional time-scale imposed by education, achievement and promotion. The father had given up at 21, Geoff a bit later. But it was hard to know what had provoked this retreat from active life: it might have been the War, more likely, it could have been Hollywood. It was difficult to find out anything positive about him. It was impossible to say whether Geoff was bored or boring, he may have been both (though the combination would be most unusual); I think it much more likely that he had found a form of serenity by living at a very low key, and spending a lot of time, like the rest of the family, including the old maid and the untidy black dog, asleep. 'Poor Geoff, my mother would say, 'he doesn't seem to get much *out* of life, he should *do* more'. My mother was an understanding woman in many ways, but total lack of ambition both puzzled her and shocked her, as flying in the face of some of her most cherished values. For she liked to be able to categorise people by achievement and promotion: an FRCS before he was 35, an LRCP at 40, a consultant at only 42 (a ladder that may also have been leaned in *my* direction; as one who took on his first salaried job at 38 – 1 made rather nonsense of her cherished hurdles). In what category to place the passive, slow-moving Geoff?

The Limbury-Buses, despite their rigid adherence to the strict time-table of regular meals, were, in the historical sense, timeless. Were they Victorians, or Edwardians, or Georgians, or even neo-Elizabethans (for all four managed to live into the present reign)? They were certainly aware of the days of the week – there was even a calendar, the gift of a local coal-merchant, hanging up in the old man's unused study, but it was unmarked, each day was a virginal blank – and of the different time-table of Sunday. Geoff and his father presumably took in the evidence of the changing seasons in the course of their routed walks. But I doubt if they could have absorbed a wider time-scale. They had lived through the twenties without being *aware* of them; it had been the same with the thirties and forties. In short, quite unconsciously, they flew in the face of history (metaphorically, of course, for even if they had had wings, they would have kept them prudently folded), mutely defying the angry historian to put them into this period or that. They may have been an extreme example of timelessness, but they were not unique in this respect, there were other people of their kind in Tunbridge Wells, though more often in *twos*: a faded old lady in pale blue and her faded old companion in pale pink, in Nevill Park; a tiny old lady, in yellowing silk, and her shrivelled, yellow-faced maid, in Hungershall Park; Miss Pohlman, my *adored* Miss Pohlman, bed-ridden and fixed permanently in a time-scale of a perpetual Tsarist Russia, and *her* companion, who, having trained as a nurse, had been able at least to take in the twenties; a *very* old General – it was said that he had served in the Crimea, and I *know* that he wore his medals at dinner – and his very old wife, and very old butler, believed once to have been his batman, in Calverley Park.

When I knew the Limbury-Buses, I was not especially conscious of being a historian. But, writing about them over a gap of nearly thirty years, it is inevitable that my angle of observation should have changed, and it is possible that I have attempted to read in their carefully closeted manner of life a number of things that were not there. Geoff and his father may have been rather stupid, as well as very idle. Their isolation may have been due to an almost total vacuity. I may have credited thoughts to people who never spent any time thinking. They may have been exceedingly unimaginative; Geoff and his father may have taken different routes to the club, either because they were fed up with one another's company, or because each found his own route the prettier and the more varied. It is possible that I have got it all completely wrong. This is a risk that any historian must run when attempting to situate people in a given place or period, or, as in the case of the Limbury-Buses, beyond both (for could it really be said that they lived in Tunbridge Wells when they saw so little of it – Mrs

Limbury-Buse, nothing beyond the thick foliage of her dark, damp garden, shrouded in evergreens?). Yet it is a risk I had to accept. Furthermore, they did not exist merely in their own right, but also in their relationship to me, as a child and as a young man. Their house was not just an object of curiosity, it also offered me a wonderfully quiet and still haven of friendliness, and, during the fears and uncertainties of War, of peace and security. I wanted everyone and everything to be *in place*. And so they would be: the china dogs on the mantelpiece, the tea-set in the corner-cupboard, the thick velvet curtains drawn, Geoff and Olive and their parents each in his or her chair, the old servant coming to the door, preceded by a strange, uneven shuffle. I never came away from the long trip up to the far end of the town – a neglected, almost forgotten one: things had moved on and away since the setting-up of the pinnacle (which was also a horse-trough, or had been once), while the trees and evergreens had grown thicker and the foliage more unkempt – without feeling happier, calmer, more at peace. The Limbury-Buses were not an object of study, a problem of long-living history, they were a restorative and a reminder of how to get one's priorities right.

As individuals, I was extremely fond of all four of them and especially of the old lady, who was kind and generous, and who always seemed pleased to see me and to hear of my activities, as an emissary from a dangerous, but perhaps exciting, outer world, beyond the ever-rising frieze of evergreens composed of holly, yew and cypress. The old man occasionally asked me questions about Paris that suggested that his knowledge of the place dated back to a vague period situated somewhere on the far side of the Commune; and I think these were simply to prevent the conversation from flagging. But he had, he said, once met a Frenchman, who was a member of the Jockey Club and who had given him a *book* (he emphasised the word as if it had been vaguely obscene); he did not know what it was about, as it was in French, but he would get it for me, if he could find it, for, as it was in French, I might like to read it; and he went off to rummage in whatever obscure corner of the house books had been confined. After about twenty minutes, he came back, with cobwebs in his white hair and with a book in a faded yellow cover, published and written in Deauville in 1921, and about the races at Longchamp, by a retired jockey. I took it away, but never read it. Old Mr Limbury-Buse was very polite, but he generally had the greatest difficulty in connecting up, once recent family news had been exhausted: your mother? Diana? Does she still play tennis? The trouble was there were only three of us, so that would not go very far. The episode of the yellow book was a rare, inspired move. But the initiative was never repeated.

I found Olive rather *jolly* – quite naturally so, for she was totally without affectation (affectation, like a change of clothing, would have required an effort) and giggly in a girlish sort of way, even when well on in her forties. She was a 'good sort', talking in what I imagine to have been the sort of language employed at St Felix or Roedean in the pre-1914 lush days of Bumper Annuals for Girls. A great many people she had known were described as 'bricks' or as 'absolutely spiffing'. Her language was eager, even energetic. Perhaps this was a hang-over from the energising ski-slopes and frozen lakes. Its crispness was in odd contrast to her father's clearly defeatist forays into conversation, as it was to her own careful conservation of energy.

Geoff had a large presence of silent gentleness. The apology for a smile seemed like a little shaft of friendliness trying to get out. But his crippling shyness made any sustained communication impossible. Perhaps the only sentence I ever heard him utter concerned the health of his father, whom I had not seen, for two or three days, at the fixed levels of his timed walks. I had pounced on Geoff outside Romary's shop, and, confronting him, had forced him into utterance: his father had a bit of a chill and was confined to bed (a slight adjustment to his normal routine). Geoff could never look – or be – angry, but his broad face took on an expression of hurt and surprise, as if I had committed an act of treachery; what is more, what with my question, and the time that it took him to answer it, I had held him up for 35 seconds, throwing his time-table out of gear. It was like deliberately getting in the way of a royal procession. I never did it again. When I met Geoff, which was quite often, as I cut across that part of the Common to attend invitations to tea, I would indicate recognition by raising my right fore-finger to the level of my head, and he would respond in the same manner. At home, his contribution to the conversation, apart from the fugitive smile, was to nod his head, very slowly, to indicate his agreement with something that had been said by his mother or by myself. He did not appear to listen when his father was speaking, and Olive's energetic flow eddied harmlessly round his large head.

I can remember so vividly every detail about my visits; I can recall the rather fuggy smell of the drawing-room, and the odour of gravy and spice that lingered in the dining-room; I could describe the exact place of the many (undusted) china objects on the mantelpiece, yet I simply cannot remember when Mr and Mrs Limbury-Buse died. I must have known some time, my mother would have written to me in Paris about their deaths. I would like to think that they died in rapid succession, and in the lifetime of their elderly maid. How either or both could have managed without her I cannot imagine; the whole economy of the household would have collapsed, the time-table would have slid into timeless chaos and they would have starved. Certainly, on one of my visits over from Paris in the early fifties, I sighted Geoff, at the correct time, at the Romary's Water Biscuits Halt; and each of the following days I had glimpses of his progress through each of the scheduled places. But I failed to spot his father anywhere along the Mount Pleasant route. I asked my mother about Geoff; she said that he seemed to be managing to cope in the empty house (Olive had gone to live in Switzerland); but I found this pretty hard to believe.

So I was greatly relieved when, on a visit ten years later, I spotted him, exactly on time, heading downhill at the level of what had been Rose Hill School and was now a block of flats. I noticed, however, that he was rather bent, that the cap had been replaced by a hat, that he was no longer wearing the plus-four suit, but what looked very much like the suit his father had worn every time I had seen him. Geoff must have been turning 70. It looked as if he would be good for another decade or more. His parents had lived well into their eighties, and Geoff had been as idle as they. Or perhaps he was no longer idle. Anything was possible; he might even have taken on the upkeep of the big, dark house, once he had found himself rattling about alone in it. He might even have discovered enjoyment in keeping it in a relatively habitable condition. The main thing was that the familiar circuit was still on. To me, it was a symbol, both of familiarity, and of continuity, like having one's own ring and one's own pigeon-hole in a small Paris restaurant, the guarantee that one could come back, and that things would be as before. I could not help admiring the Limbury-Buses for their rigorous attachment to routine, and their sunny ability in insulating themselves from everything disagreeable or threatening that came in from outside.

12 DOORS AND WINDOWS

In the course of my walks, at whatever time of day, I would pass many front-doors behind which I had penetrated; and thus I came to see Tunbridge Wells as consisting of a series of interlocking privacies, a mingling of addresses at fixed times, and according to unstated, but recognised, conventions. There could be a proper time for the drawbridge to be brought down and for a carefully restricted breach of privacy. One would not expect to gain entry through a front-door – unless it was that of a doctor or a dentist – in the morning, or at any time much before 3. People did not ask one another to lunch, though they might arrange to meet at lunch – as they might meet for morning coffee at the Cadena or the Tudor Café – in one of those establishments that seem to have marked the thirties and that served modest, three-course Southern English meals by well-spoken ladies, generally in couples, and wearing artistic smocks over their tweeds, to show that they were not servants. The same establishments could later double up for tea. And tea was the principal occasion for social intercourse, for getting beyond the front-door – my interior topography of Tunbridge Wells was situated between 4 and 6, and mostly in daylight (save at the Limbury-Buses') so that one could take in all the details. But organised penetration of specified areas of the groundfloor interior could also be carried out between tea and 6.30 or 7. Bridge could provide access even after supper.

How little, too, the *windows* would give away! Behind the frieze of lace curtains objects could only be dimly seen or hinted at: the vague outline of a book-case or of a stand-up piano, the dull gleam of a brass pot, the diffuse pink light, on a portion of ceiling thrown by an elaborate lamp-shade its tasselled fringe also projected on the ceiling, moving and swirling in a variety of shades and announcing to the overcoated passer-by the warmth and comfort of a piled-up coal fire, or a seated cat on a window-sill thrown into regular moving silhouette, as it licked a back paw held in mutton-chop position, by the filtered brightness behind it. Then windows were designed to look out of – discreetly, of course – not to look *in* through, were concerned to protect privacy, not to arrest the passer-by and cause him to stop in contemplation of an intimate domestic scene. At very most, there might be provided a brief, plunging view, suddenly illuminating right back to the far wall and throwing its inmates into sharp relief, as, after turning on the light, they set about, drawing the heavy curtains, in an act as much to cut out the intrusive exterior as to cut out the cold. For well over thirty years, the uneven line of lighted windows facing us from across Claremont Road at roughly the level of our kitchen or our dining-room never revealed anything of the slightest interest, but merely the nature of this room or that: a bedroom, its function suggested by the oblong shadow thrown by a dressing-table mirror, a kitchen, which had nothing to conceal, because one spent so little time in it and was always in a hurry to get out of it, a bright, bare place, briefly illuminated, in cold, unblinking light, and as rapidly plunged back into the dark void, as if to announce, from across the street, an indifference to gastronomy assumed to be generally shared. It would have been a sort of mild affront if the bright kitchen had remained in full naked view for more than a few minutes, and a serious cause for concern if the bright glare in the night had gone on shining quite unashamedly, throwing a thin line of yellow light across the silent road, and revealing the presence of several seated figures, for a kitchen was a place to stand up in, rather furtively, as if the gestures engaged in over the sink were somewhat shameful. The lighted windows would also reveal to those opposite the absence of a living-in maid, an absence that one would not wish to publicise, though it would be easy enough to discern. Most of the houses in Claremont Road could only run to dailies (only the Weekes', old Mr Evans, and Miss Vian, the sister of an Admiral, enjoying the luxury of maintaining a resident maid). What a cause for alarm would have been the brazen revelation of seated figures in a kitchen, *eating*! What sort of people were these? It would have been as if the reassuring negative signals exchanged from across the chasm of the dark road – *their* kitchen light responding in brief acknowledgment, and at the same reasonable early hour, – had broken down, or had been abandoned. The bathroom, too, would announce itself through pebbled glass. There might be tacitly authorised exceptions: a child's room, the child sitting near the window, sucking a pencil, in front of an open exercise book, a map of the world and some cycling pennants on the wall, a revolving globe on the table. But little more.

What, for that matter, did we or our neighbours do about washing? I don't think I ever thought about the question at the time, or that I was aware of something not being there which one would have expected to have been there. I could have walked the whole of Tunbridge Wells without catching sight of such a thing. Perhaps it was hidden away in invisible back-gardens; I *think* our line was on the flat roof, set at an angle which would have made it impossible to see from the level of the road. I realise now that a washing line would have given away much too much: the presence of an extra inhabitant, whether male or female, the fact that the same pair of pyjamas, or the same nightdress made their public appearances at too great frequency, or, on the contrary, at a frequency too spaced out – indicating either that they were often not worn for nights on end, or that those who *did* wear them were not particularly fussy about cleanliness. It would be the same with sheets – too often out, the suggestion of sin; too seldom out, the hint of an Irish presence. Or the sheets and pillow-cases might be seen to be torn, the shorts or trousers might be seen to have been patched, the collars of the shirts might be seen to have been turned. Visible clothes-lines would have indicated that those who put them up did not care about what people thought: pirates' signals hanging insolently in Claremont Road.

In all those years, not one single glimpse of domestic intimacy, even momentarily revealed. My mother (and Mrs Martin, or my mother through Mrs Martin) would know the names of 'the people living opposite'; she would even know what they did, how many children and animals they had, whether or not they had a car. She might even greet them in the street. But that would be as far as it would go. There was really no point in looking out of the window, on the street side, for there was nothing to see. No one looked out of the window, it would have been too suggestive: to lean out, for instance, in the direction of the corner of Claremont Road and Grove Hill, as if waiting to see when the postman turned into the road, could imply that one was awaiting a postal order, or, if the husband had already gone to work, that one was hoping for a letter of an intimate kind and that one would carry away to read upstairs in the seclusion of the bedroom. Or it could be just about legitimate to do so round about 5 o'clock, in order to ascertain whether one of the children was on time on the way back from school; and even a display of such concern might be considered as rather ostentatious and out of place: a somewhat alien display of anxiety, the suggestion of a propensity to *fuss*. For everyone knew that children would make their own way back in their own time.

I am, of course, speaking of the late-twenties and the thirties. The War, while imposing black-out curtains, would at once bring many breaches into a previously observed discretion and to a mutually respected privacy. Many doors would be opened, to admit many visitors previously unthinkable. As the main ARP warden of the upper end of Claremont Road, my mother gained frequent admission to every house in the street. Temporarily, doors and windows became less jealously guarded, small front-rooms, and even rooms upstairs, yielding up their harmless secrets. No wonder my mother enormously enjoyed the War years; for the first – and last – time, she felt herself part of the street, and discovered that tradesmen and shopkeepers could be not only acceptable as neighbours, but also interesting and friendly individuals, with their own specific skills and hobbies. But, once the War was over, everyone went back to the position as before, and, while the black-out curtains came down, the windows regained their blindness, by day and by night, and the doors their relative impenetrability. My mother thought it was a pity, and was distressed when she found out that some of her neighbours seemed embarrassed when she stopped to talk to them in the road. But she soon gave up. It was as if all involved were concerned to forget what had happened, what they had seen: all those front – and back-rooms that they had entered, all the intimate objects that they had been unable to help noticing, in corner cupboards or on mantelpieces, all the willing exchanges of skills and services. Within weeks, things were back to where they had been in 1939, my mother reduced to the three houses in the road that had opened their doors to her. Even those who returned from the Forces, once they had discarded their uniforms and put on civilian clothes, put on with them the high fences and thick curtains of privacy and discretion, and fell back, unquestioning, into all the tacit assumptions of a community that politely pretended to look the other way, so as not to be embarrassing, and to walk on its toes, so as not to make too much noise. In a way, it was rather reassuring, such ready common acceptance – as if in response to a secret signal – of old personal and family values of privacy, indicating what little impact the five horrible years of collective public perils, of enforced promiscuity, of fear, panic and unease had had on a middle-class community in which the prime concern of everyone was to keep to himself or herself, and not to step beyond the very limited standards of a cautious and restricted sociability.

Windows, then, gave nothing away and carried no messages, save the quite frequent *To Let* notices (one hardly ever saw *For Sale* ones) and the capital letters *C.P.*, in red, on a green background, that would be put prominently in the window for a few days, to be removed later. I did not know what Carter Paterson, the origin of the initials, *did*, or why one should thus solicit a call from one of their employees.

There were also a few *Bed & Breakfast* signs displayed on windows, but well off my usual routes, down the lower reaches of Upper Grosvenor Road. I was told about them first by a red-haired boy who went to Rose Hill and who lived down that way. He managed to convince me that the emphasis should be on the former word (not at all in an innocent or purely functional sense, that 'all sorts of things went on' in the upper rooms of such places: he pointed out to me, when I went with him to see for myself, that some of the signs were actually displayed in the *upper* window, making the meaning clearer) and that breakfast was really only a pretext, a camouflage for what went before. Certainly, the breakfast décor look unappetising and jaded, at least as seen at 5, when we were pursuing our rather breathless investigation of wickedness down Upper Grosvenor Road: a cruet that was not made of silver, a bottle of HP sauce, little pink paper napkins done up like fans, a saucer of marmalade in which a fly had drowned, and a packet of Force laid out on a forlorn and stained whitish table-cloth, four washable place-mats (that hadn't been washed for some time) put out ready for the two guilty couples the place could accommodate. Would the couples speak to one another, over the second-*B*, or would they keep their noses well down in the plates of Force? Sin certainly looked very sordid and rather seedy. Even so, my redhead friend, Elliott, and I enjoyed the *frisson* of prying in on the table set for four for the next morning, when it would all be over. One result of our close observation of no. 61a was to associate sin with goldfish and artificial flowers. Anyhow it excited us to give *B & B* the suggestion of sulphur. The reality was no doubt less sinful but equally banal. Certainly, Tunbridge Wells was not a place to which families went for their summer holidays – it was too near the coast – so the *B & B* cards were more likely to have been for the attention of commercial travellers and men in double-breasted suits who went from door to door in too highly polished shoes and trying to sell vacuum cleaners. So the reality of no. 61a – and of similar places further down the road – would not be two guilty couples pretending not to see one another, but four men in striped suits reading the *Daily Mail* and the *Daily Mirror* over breakfast, after sleeping, two upstairs, and two downstairs: the one on a folding bed in the back-room facing onto the tiny yard, the other on a bed convertible into a couch in the front-room, the scene of our eager investigation of the supposed aftermath of conventional sin as spied from outside through a protruding window and not very white lace curtains.

13 THE OBSERVATORY

In such a secretive and unrevealing place there would be much to be said for looking at things from the wrong side; the view of the back could reveal aspects stripped of pretensions. The back did not have to bother with keeping up appearances, though this would not be the case with the view from inside *onto* the back, as seen, in between drilling activities, from the dentist's chair; then the back would have to be neat and reassuring: a well-kept, well-rolled lawn and two impeccable borders, and perhaps a small statue, a bird-bath, or a sundial, to focus the eye and emphasise the perspective, at the end. The garden view was designed to take the mind off the agonies of the drill and the apprehension of its return, as the long arm was pulled down into position at mouth level, so that, in Tunbridge Wells, behind the Regency houses on Mount Ephraim or on St John's Road, the dentists had the best-kept gardens; they were not for sitting in – and *when* did a dentist have time to sit down? – but only for looking at. Of course, they were *too* neat and tidy; there was something menacing and functional about those carefully blended clumps of flowers, blue down one border, pink and red down the other. It was rather like having the torture chambers lined in washable tiles. There was something *furtive*, too, about those back gardens, as viewed from the ground floor or the first floor, as if what went on in the rooms that overlooked them had to be on the discreet garden side, and screened from the street. Who ever heard of a dentist's surgery in a front room? Or, if such ever existed, it would have been that of a pretty poor quality dentist. Certainly, in the years of childhood and adolescence, and a score or so of those that followed, I had viewed perhaps thirty or more such long, enclosed gardens, from various levels, starting from the back of Hungershall Park, then taking in the backs of Mount Ephraim, then the dank, dripping gardens of Ferndale, the strips of lawn behind the busy road to Southborough, then, *in extremis*, a small, rather humble garden, but still neat, off one of the little roads that led off the Common. I had not quite completed the Grand Tour of dental chairs; but I had swung round in a wide arc, almost a complete semi-circle, taking in the western perimeter of the town, the afternoon sun pouring into the dental chambers and offering additional help to the white-coated figures as they excavated with tiny picks among the blackening ruins of my mouth. It hadn't been a continuing arc; I had jumped to and fro, back and forth, avoiding the heavy-handed and in search of the light gentle pull. But my movements here and there across the backs reproduced, on a much larger scale the swivels from side to side and backward, upright and forward, of the chair itself. Of course, in a long career of decay and deterioration, I had viewed a great many back gardens in other towns, and even the dark grey courtyards of Parisian apartment blocks – the gardens seem to have been a purely English dental refinement – but it was in Tunbridge Wells that I had gathered together the most extensive collection of backs ranging from lupins to gladioli, from red-hot pokers to rhododendrons, from brilliant roses to pinks and carnations, from privet and box, to ivy and evergreen. Occasionally, there would be movement in the still, trim gardens; a robin, or a well-fed dental cat, stretched out, and basking in the sun. But never a bench, or a deck-chair, always an enclosed rectangular landscape without figures.

But, in one particular, quite exceptional instance, the view *from* the back was both unedifying, unstudied, untidy, and yet highly informative, indeed a talking map, a high observatory onto what was supposed to be hidden. This was from the barber's chair in a room upstairs – high up, second or third floor – at Weekes', and that faced onto the semi-made-up road that ran parallel to Mount Pleasant and that was used by dustmen when they came to remove the bins, and, on summer evenings, by couples who wished to avoid the public stare of the steep shopping street. I enjoyed the barber's chair as much as the thought of the elaborate dental chair, with its pedals and its silver handles, filled me with (justified) foreboding. Even if a final visit to the barber's chair would announce the imminence of Term and my consequent departure from the freedom and solitary enjoyment of Tunbridge Wells, I could still look forward to the visit to Weekes', while the *first* visit there after Term would offer a double attraction: the realisation of the beginning of the holidays and of all the days of freedom lying ahead, and the opportunity to catch up on what had been going on during my absence. The interest was not in the view – one was' scarcely aware of that – but came from behind and up above, not far from the back of one's head. Did one go to the hairdresser's more often in the twenties and thirties, when short hair prevailed, at the behest both of parents and of schools, and when the full treatment – including shampoo, neck-massage, spray, and beyond childhood, shave – cost little, than in the present, more hirsute decade? It may be so, for, certainly, I have memories of sitting upstairs at Weekes', waiting my turn among a row of seated, grey-jerseyed, grey-shirted, grey-flannelled, grey-socked figures perhaps as much as once a fortnight. At whatever time in the holidays, the visits to the backroom upstairs, with its indifferent view onto the dirt-road, provided the best possible source of information about the more secret goings-on occurring in the Royal Borough, even though the wonderfully talkative and benign-*looking* (for he wasn't benign) old man, with a shock of white hair and with philosophical rimless spectacles, faced the wrong way, away from Mount Pleasant and onto the generally deserted road. So it was not *visual* evidence that had made him the salacious onlooker of some of the secrets of the younger population of the town. Perhaps he acted as a sort of standing-up confessor to his small armies of red-haired, curly-haired, dark-haired, fair-haired, greasy-haired, grey-jerseyed seated customers, as the two-way talk carried on between the sound of scissors clipping; perhaps people actually talked from the tops of their heads. The volume of information that he could provide was prodigious. Nor was it all engagingly scandalous. Elliott (not Master Elliott) had had a new bicycle, with saddle-bags, a horn, and a speedometer. Pearmund was in bed with measles. Cotta had a black eye so he had been in the wars again. I was glad to hear this; I would have been still gladder if Cotta had had two black eyes, for he had knocked me down and I had split my head on a wash-basin at Rose Hill; Farrell had got into Eton, young de la Warr had *not* got into Oxford, though his father was a Minister. Featherstone was so clever with his hands; Palmer had won a dancing prize. A pity about Douglas, his parents breaking up. Poor Munro, his father had gone bankrupt.

One would have expected him to be well-informed about the doings of the boy population, and about boy and parent relations; he even seemed to have been able to read the full details of school reports – Greek or conduct – out of hair. Of course, we all chatted away to him between clips, with joyful abandon and with not a little embroidering, in the certain knowledge that it would all be passed on to the back of the next head in the chair, which would then provide him with a further stock of information, to be passed on in its turn, a sort of relay-race of gossip, bragging, mild malice, knowing giggles, and very broad hints. So it was easy to see his information bank in week-day upstair operation, from 10 to 5, with an hour off for lunch (when, as well as eating, he no doubt digested and catalogued the morning's pickings, as they fell, from young chattering mouths as did the hair, in various shades, on the floor). Schoolboy heads presented no problem, they were hardly a challenge, all he had to do was to set the machine in motion, by a comment, a question, or a bit of base flattery, and they would gabble away happily to an orchestra of snorts and giggles coming from the waiting audience. He was regarded by middle-class parents – foolish middle-class parents – as the best hairdresser in town, and he must have cut the hair of two or three decades of schoolboys in his time. He seemed old to me, but, from subsequent evidence, I think he was about midway in his career as the town gossip and confessor when I was at the Beacon and at Shrewsbury. I believe he had another twenty years of clipping and listening still ahead of him. Certainly, when home from Paris, I would make a point of going upstairs in order to catch up on the interrupted chronicle, though it would now relate to an adolescent population ten years or more behind me. But he was also remarkably successful in keeping some tabs on his former customers in whose subsequent careers he seemed to take a genuine interest.

What was the true measure of his worth was the realisation – which would come at one's very first sitting – that though he never came into close range of *female* heads, never clipped, combed, or washed *female* hair, never swept up *female* clippings, he was equally *au fait* with all the fortunes and misfortunes of the other, mysterious half of the childhood and adolescent population. He could put a name and an address onto any girl broadly described, and could then fill in on family background, schooling, conduct, and, for those bolder than myself, prepared to set foot on these alien shores, sexual inclinations. A 'looker', yes, but it was deceptive, nothing doing. 'As if butter would not melt in her mouth, but . . . the bushes on the Common . . .'. Could it have been that he had a colleague or a wife who worked on the heads of the other half? I never discovered; but the information was there for the asking. He seemed well up with my sister's current boy-friends. Often I would first hear about them upstairs, before they actually appeared at the house, or, wearing blazers, in a boat on the Medway. But his real speciality was doctors' daughters.

He had a very long run, in his upstair verbal observatory, and he was always generous with his information. He was a sharer rather than a secret collector, and one could be sure always of coming away with something. My mother, who professed herself indifferent to gossip, would listen with the hint of a smile, to whatever I had to bring home from Weekes'. She did not seem to doubt the accuracy of the reports and would sometimes comment: 'Of course, I could have told them . . .', making herself wise after the event. She never actually met the Artist himself, trusting me to relay to him such instructions as I had been given regarding my hair (there was nothing much that even the Artist could do about the way it stood up in obstinate tufts at the crown) with particular emphasis on having it shaved at the back of the neck. But she knew him by repute; his fame – and much of his information – had reached the Bridge tables. I suppose, in the end, he retired. I went to Weekes' once and was confronted by a stranger who, while clipping, never opened his mouth. He was an exception. Later, I would listen, at back of head level, to the flow of words in French or Italian, or in Mr Germer's broken English, myself contributing as best I could (not very well in Italian) to the engaging sociability of the sweet-smelling saloon. I think the reason that my mother, at a time when her very fine hair had become very thin, persisted in going down the hill for her fortnightly visits to 'Elaine', was to keep up with what was going on. When she came back up the hill, her thinning hair would have been 'done', in a style suited to her age; but she would also provide a verbal column on Births, Deaths, Marriages, Accidents, Misfortunes, and Burst Pipes. Much later, I went to a hairdresser's opposite the Calverley Hotel; he was very friendly, and would break off every now and then, in full sentence, to sell French letters to customers not concerned for the moment with hair. I thought it represented a curious combination of skills and trades, almost as bizarre as the French *bougnat*: *Vins Charbons*. But the Artist upstairs in Weekes' was in a class of his own. There is something else I can remember about him now; he always wore a winged collar, while officiating as a standing confessor, but without a tie.

14 THE WAR MEMORIAL

When I grew up, Tunbridge Wells tended to become a place of refuge from sentimental storms experienced elsewhere, yet it had not been quite loveless; there were three girls, two of them sisters, whom I had admired, in a vague sort of way, and very much from afar, during the early months of the 'phoney war', and possibly as a means of passing the time and helping to fill the vacuum of *waiting* during that strange period of ominous silence and indecision – an indecision on a scale both national and personal, a sort of uneasy holiday, taken without permission, yet not expressly forbidden, during which so many people were thrown on their own devices: 'you are not needed now, but you may be later'. I knew roughly where the three girls lived, but I did not know their exact addresses, and had never got as far as window-watching; I just found them agreeable to encounter and to look at over coffee at elevenses. Later, when the War in Europe ended, I brought one of them a pair of silk stockings over from Brussels (where one could obtain anything): she had not yet been demobilised, and was working as manageress of a canteen in Eastbourne. I went over there with the stockings, and we walked up and down the Front for an afternoon, before the canteen reopened and I took the train back to Tunbridge Wells. The relationship, timid and tentative, and based on a feeling of friendship and a shared amusement at some of the more bizarre conventions accepted by the Bridge-playing inhabitants of her neighbourhood, never got beyond such exchanges. She had a boy friend in London who had worked for the BBC before the War and who was now engaged on some ultra-secret Intelligence operations involving occupied Europe; and we used to talk about him and what he did – she seemed to be fully informed – when we met during my intermittent leaves. She must have had influence well beyond the limits of the canteen in Eastbourne, for, as the result of a

The War Memorial

chance expression of interest on my part, the boy friend rapidly
put me in the way of people who arranged for, generally single,
trips to France; I had a number of interviews at addresses in St
John's Wood, South Kensington and Mayfair. But it never got
beyond that, neither the relationship, nor the trip; I was quite
happy for the former to remain on a footing of friendly
familiarity, while, in the course of one of the interviews – not
the final one – I openly expressed doubts about my own
suitability for work in occupied territory; I did not think I was
brave enough for this sort of thing. A throw-away remark, made
on the way to her home at the top end of the town, at the *exact*
level of Tunbridge Wells War Memorial – there was nothing at
all in the association, the moonlit statue, in puttees, and
weighed down with the full infantry gear, spelling out the very
different priorities of a previous War, and holding out a bayonet
pointed in the direction of Holy Trinity and the Common – had
set in motion the vast and mysterious apparatus of one of the
Secret Services. I wondered afterwards whether things often
happened in this rather casual way. It was yet another example
of the casual and quite unpredictable interlocking of public and
private lives that seems so often to have occurred during the
War years. Tunbridge Wells was more important than might
have appeared on first sight, especially when one of its more
desirable female inhabitants had a boy friend who had worked
for the jazz programme of the BBC. Perhaps, after all, this had
been the secret vocation of the place, under the entirely
reassuring cover of its long-established middle-class respectability. It was a sobering thought that, had I not suddenly
applied the brakes and prudently got out, I might have found
myself travelling on a switch-back route towards a topography
that bore no resemblance to the modest and domesticated
gothicity of the High Rocks, reachable beyond their large,
cast-iron turnstyle. There was no doubt in my mind that the
High Rocks, approached beyond the turnstile, by paths of
stone steps, represented my own prudent dimension. I was not

107

aspiring to a stained-glass window in Shrewsbury School chapel. Bridget had probably been quite unaware of the consequences of my chance expression of dissatisfaction at having to teach Czech soldiers English, when my French might have been used to better profit to the War effort; perhaps I had been trying to impress her; or it may be that I had been temporarily afflicted with a mood of Byronic romanticism quite alien to my own temperament. *Of course* I was much better off teaching the Czechs English than engaging in some madcap outfit. It had been a quite uncharacteristic outburst. I am sure she was quite unaware of what she was about to set in motion, when she had promised, under the stony gaze of the over-loaded soldier, ready to defend the Common against foreign invasion, 'to have a word with Eric about me'.

So our relationship – despite the sudden shove that she had almost casually given to the possible course of my wartime career (which would soon have ended at a terminus if I had allowed it to proceed on the gathering momentum of the shove) – remained what it had always been; it did not involve any claim on an indeterminate future. Eric seems to have gone the way of so many wartime boy friends. And, some time later, in her anxiety to leave the parish of St John's and its rather restricting boundaries, she married a man much older than herself, a headmaster of a primary school, and went to live in Hong Kong. This was not as complete an escape as she might have hoped, for she soon encountered there a dozen or so fellow-Tunbridge Wellsians, refugees not so much from the place as from an austere Labourite England. Eventually she herself became a good Bridge player – quite up to the standards of her parents' parish – but in the climate of the Colony she soon lost her good looks.

I suppose there were plenty of other attractive girls about when I was a schoolboy or an undergraduate; but I never seemed to meet any, mainly, I suppose, because I did not take part in any of the collective activites that were available to my age group. There was a poetry society that met in a room upstairs over the far end of the Pantiles, but I only went to it once – the pretty girls were not there, and I was not very interested in poetry. I did not play tennis, and only went to the sort of pubs likely to be frequented by retired coachmen, butlers and family retainers who had been in the service of the Nevills, the Pratts and the Sidneys or of local medical dynasties, or of former Ladies-in-Waiting to Queen Alexandra. At Oxford, I went to ugly mock-Tudor pubs with my scout – the height of social acceptance in the curiously inverted thirties; and there one would play shove-ha'penny with other scouts. There was very briefly on the scene a blonde girl, a nurse from Aylesbury Infirmary, but I panicked when matters seemed to be proceeding too fast for my liking. As far as I was concerned, Tunbridge Wells and sex did not reside together. At the most, I would have to make do with the flat, unsubstantial paper services of photographs in *Men Only* (very Lonely Men), of nude French girls displaying themselves on inviting sand-dunes. Thin fare, indeed, offering only momentary satisfaction.

So, as I grew from adolescence, window-watching had no great attraction for me; nor was I the least bit curious about the possible location of a local Lesbos and of a Boyne Park Sodom. Such thoughts never occurred to me at the time, because they would have been unthinkable. The thirties, as experienced in a middle-class town in the South of England, were no doubt not more innocent – they were probably *less* innocent – than later decades, but they were more discreet, more private, and, thus, much more *exciting*. I was a very secretive person, both at home and at school; and the certain knowledge of sin could best be savoured alone and behind closed doors. Sin openly indulged in and flaunted would have been very dull indeed. Or this was how I – a very timid soul – viewed the matter. Privacy, semi-privacy, and controlled breaches of privacy, offering a limited view of the interior, were thus carefully regulated by a well-calculated system of rationing designed to exclude from outside observation anything at all unseemly: family rows or conjugal uproars could be assigned to non-visiting hours. Perhaps that was why mornings were inviolate; more likely, they had to be used for getting ready for the afternoons. The securities of middle-class life in Tunbridge Wells were maintained by a careful balance between isolation and sociability.

But, even *after* the War, outside events occasionally continued to intrude on domestic privacy, breaking in, as with a sledge-hammer, into the most cherished and highly polished interiors. There was the dreadful case of my friend Peter, also a cousin of the Limbury-Buses, a boy with a terrible stammer five or six years younger than myself (so I was not unique in the misfortune of having been born too early or too late). Peter was the only son of a Bridge-playing couple. He and his mother and father lived in a large mock-Tudor house – 1910 or so, one of the best, still lavish periods of Tunbridge Wells domestic architecture – near St John's, and not very far from Bridget and the Limbury-Buses (possibly they wished to remain within easy walking distance of their tramlike cousins). Poor Peter, apart from the stammer, was in blooming health, so he had to do his National Service. There was no way of getting him out of it; everything had been tried, including an oblique approach to the medical board in Maidstone; even the MP had proved powerless. He was offered the choice of serving in one of the Forces or of going down a *mine* – and, though the War was over, and the Forces seemed relatively *safe* – he actually opted for the latter. He went down a mine somewhere in the far north of the country, in an area the existence of which barely impinged on the consciousness of most Tunbridge Wellsians, save perhaps as the sort of place the cloth-capped hunger-marchers started off from. But he was soon back, quite shattered, pale and drawn, and stammering more than ever. It had – he said to me, lowering his voice, in between stammers, in awe – been absolutely *awful*: the digs, the food, something called High Tea and involving no silver and thinly-cut cucumber sandwiches, getting up early in the morning, often in the dark, washing in a tin bath, the actual working conditions, the noise and the heat, above all, the language and the attitudes of his work-mates; they had made fun of his accent, had ribbed him incessantly, had taken him out to the pub and made him drink *beer*, had introduced him to large, buxom, red-faced girls with elaborate hair-styles, and they had never heard of Tunbridge Wells ('what did they make there?'). He seemed completely crushed. Strings were pulled, this time with more success. He was released from the mines and went into the Army after all, soon getting a commission in quite a good regiment, and continuing to stammer. He actually *enjoyed* the Army; but it left him as shy and as apologetic about himself as ever. Then he joined the Cannon Street contingent and wore a bowler hat over his dark curly hair; but the City did not suit him, nor did the heartiness of the red-faced, watery-blue-eyed 5.50 bar-supporters; so it was decided that he should stay at home. He did that for some years, not doing anything else very much but playing a lot of Bridge – not at the Club, the crowd there made him nervous – but on the mixed Bridge-playing circuit. He was a partner much in demand with the more accomplished and inveterate female players, who appreciated his manners and felt rather motherly towards him. My mother liked him very much – such a considerate, polite young man, always ready with the advanced chair or to take one's coat. She also said he was one of the best players in the town; and she would certainly know. I expect he's still living in his parents' house; I cannot imagine him anywhere else. He may even have got rid of his stammer; he was taking elocution lessons at one time, in an effort to do so.

15 FIGURES IN A LANDSCAPE

It has been a very long, very circuitous journey so far, attempting to explore Tunbridge Wells from every angle by every means. I have tried front-doors and back-doors, I have taken the fashionable Parks, as they face onto their ample, grassy meadows, breathed the air of Mount Ephraim, cut down the narrow alley-ways that run behind the little houses parallel to Claremont Road and in which the dustbins are kept – middle-class *traboules* that provided one, as a nine-year-old, convenient escape routes, and exciting, dark journeys between high wooden fences and fast-moving cats. I have enjoyed the panorama of the town from the top of the Wellington Rocks. Then I have narrowed Tunbridge Wells to a single location: my mother's house. Its confusing address made it more difficult to track us down, and this, I felt, was a distinct advantage; the more difficult, the better, unknown visitors generally meaning trouble. The house, too, I have approached from every possible angle, walking on the pavements in red and bluish-grey bricks, on the round pebbles of Little Mount Sion, cutting through along the concrete paths of the Grove, or taking the more fashionable, most impressive approach (though the final destination would, by contrast, be something of a let-down) through Calverley Park. I have spent some time – as I generally had to – on the slopes of Grove Hill.

I have explored the interior of the house floor by floor (only two); but I have forgotten the tin and green canvas tropical trunks, marked, in large white letters, THE HYTHE, in the box-room leading onto the flat roof, and I have omitted the outline of a face in profile, with a large nose, of a man walking, discernible on the inside of the lavatory door, and, despite several coats of paint and several successive layers of brown varnish, still walking, right through my childhood and adolescence and through my thirties and forties, always a figure

112

of reassurance, almost a friend, discernible, I liked to think, only to myself, who could read the message of the cracks in the wood. I felt like giving him a wave, or some form of greeting and recognition, if only to let him know that I had seen him, that I appreciated his fidelity in never missing a day, never slacking, always walking, from left to right, and so facing resolutely towards Birdcage Walk and the bowling green, but never getting to either. He had walked right through the dreadful War, and, like myself, had come out the other side of it, from Warsaw to VJ Day, faithful little *compagnon de route*. I knew that he was endeavouring to reassure me, to show me that everything was as before and would go on being so, and trying to take off the chilly sharpness of the days of fear in between. After a long absence, I would find him there to greet me. I hope too that he, like Johnny Walker, still resists new coats of paint, to go on walking, even though unseen by those seated facing his profile. For lavatories and the strange marks on their doors or their walls, constitute the secret places in which is guarded the spirit of a house, the trusted companion of a secure childhood. The sight of my little walking man gave me the same sense of familiar childish pleasure as that of the gurgling bubbles of an underwater disturbance rising up to the surface and provoked by a powerful fart, or by that of a little yellowing cascade, resulting from similar underwater activities while in the bath.

I have explored as many other interiors as I was able to penetrate and I could enumerate every item in gentle Miss Fleetwood's ground-floor museum to her Cromwellian ancestor (whom, in her family piety, she seemed to have regarded as gentle as herself) in the small drawing-room of her house right on the sharp bend of Claremont Road. And I have attempted to set my mother's house in the surrounding landscape, describing the view from it at different times of the day or the night (when the line of yellow lights went on to indicate the length of Mount Ephraim as seen from my bedroom window). In the course of much apparently aimless wandering, I have added in those

113

whom I encountered the most often, so that, in the course of time, they became inseparable from the places at which they could be the most regularly sighted. For I have wished to introduce not just a town, but some of the people in it. These I have brought in more or less in the order in which they turned up, not in terms of class or occupation, but in those of normal or at least credible location. I would not think of placing Geoff Limbury-Buse on Grove Hill, not because he disdained it, but because he had never been *near* it, and had probably never heard of it, as of so much else. *Had* he ever heard of it, he would have learned that it was too steep for him to manage. None of the Limbury-Buses had ever been to see my mother; they had no car, and it was out of the question to attempt such a journey on foot. It was up to my mother to go and see *them* (on foot). I suppose it was some sort of a compliment to her that a great many people – not just her cousins – tended to make just such assumptions on the subject of my mother. It was assumed, for instance, that she liked walking because she was seen to do a great deal of it, often over quite long distances. It did not always occur to them that she did not possess a car. Still, I believe she was rather pleased that people would take such things for granted in respect of her; she had such a horror of those who, though in good health, never put a foot out-of-doors: a sign of weakness and self-indulgence as condemnable as sleeping with the bedroom window shut.

I would not think of placing the Black Widow on Claremont Road; she might not even have been noticed there, or only been observed from behind lace curtains; and it was rather a humble, quite undramatic thoroughfare, totally un-Gothic and not coming up to the requirements of such an excessive display of permanent grief – or so she may have thought, for plenty of (restrained) grief resided here discreetly, on and off, jumping three or four of the little houses at a time, to settle on this one or that, taking up temporary residence in it. Mr Weekes' long black limousines were as much at home in Claremont Road as in

Broadwater Down, the rival firm of Hickmott had already begun its steady advance up much of the left side of Grove Hill, death not observing the many subtle social distinctions that seem to have been so important to my mother and to many of her friends (a Claremont Road address would not look well on a visiting-card, would not open doors in the Parks, but there were other considerations that could mitigate the effects of a bad address; my aunt had been able to vouch for my mother – from the time of our arrival in 1921 – and a doctor's daughter would go right up to the top, whatever her address). In the last stages of my father's illness, an iron rail had been placed the whole length of the outside steps that gave access to the house, to help him up or down in his extreme weakness (he had been both down and up the day before he died). His death must have imposed unusual problems to the strong men in black from Weekes' or Hickmott's for the coffin would have to have been brought down, at a considerable angle, the same way, so that his death must have been more widely known than most.

It would have been unthinkable to have placed the melancholy seller of the *Argus* anywhere other than outside the Great Hall, for that location – airless in summer, damp and foggy in winter – seemed to constitute the limit of his only known world, though he must have come from somewhere else. The kilted Scot *lived* on the Common and was never seen in the town, though he must sometimes have shopped somewhere. The bearded ex-officer hermit in greyish cricket trousers and damp, derelict blazer, greening at the edges, ranged down from his tented headquarters in a field by the Hawkenbury Corner to Claremont Road and Calverley Park, where his upper-class accent gave him an extensive custom for his boxes of matches and bootlaces that he would have been unable to attract on the lower slopes of Grove Hill; and he was never sighted further down, so must have done such shopping as he required in Hawkenbury. A retired archdeacon – one of the walking wonders of my childhood, because he had a wireless in his hat and wore gaiters – could be firmly consigned to the neighbourhood of the West Station, as well as to the Orange Tea Rooms, where I once saw him, sitting alone at a table, eating muffins; he was quite bald, with a polished shiny head. The buckle shoes and the gaiters had never carried him and the hat with struts and wires up Mount Sion, Little Mount Sion or Grove Hill. It would have been imprudent, too, to have sent Mr Weekes, an old man of absolutely fixed habits that had enabled him to live (with his unmarried sister) so long (they both reached their middle-nineties, dying within a month of one another – *two* visits from his own black limousines) to the top of Mount Ephraim, just as it would have been unimaginable to have located any of the fashionable dentists anywhere other than there. Miss Amy Lake seldom got much beyond the far end of the Pantiles – a visit to Jupps' sweet-shop – to buy snuff for herself and sweets for her pupils. It would have been a bold act of imagination to have picked her (and her black-and-white fox-terrier) up and to have put them down in the vicinity of the Wellington Rocks. Mrs Coad's brown daimler was seen in Claremont Road – 'slumming' for me – at the beginning and the end of term. The chauffeur could never find it on his own, even after eleven such journeys, so that he had to be instructed how to get there by Mrs Coad, through the speaking-tube. My resentment at the willingness – not to say the eagerness – shown by my mother to enter into such obligations, even to seek them out, was thus further compiled by embarrassment at having caused them both so much trouble. The twice-termly appearance of the majestic slow-moving car must have caused a small sensation in that observant road.

My aunt Emily's locations were entirely predictable and were concentrated in a very limited area (save during the First World War when she had been matron of a Base hospital somewhere in France which took in French as well as British casualties): one of them was the hospital, near the top of Mount Sion, where she lived; another our house in Claremont Road – the extreme limit of her movements on foot – which she visited several times a week, on the stroke of lunch. She would sit at a corner of the lunch-table in her black admiral's hat and fur coat and with her gloves on, as if she were only looking in for a moment ('I am only looking in for a moment'). After refusing to have any lunch, saying that she never ate at that time of the day, she would watch *us* eat, rather clinically, making all four of us feel slightly guilty, and causing me to spill even more than usual. She would sit right through lunch, asking questions and commenting on the appearance of the food ('Dora, I think you should change your butcher', 'where did you get those plums? they look rather *blown* to me', 'you need to be so careful what you give to a growing child'). She always stayed to the end, refusing coffee. After she retired from the hospital, she moved to a flat just beyond the bottom of Mount Sion, in the Kentish Mansions – rather dingy mansions – overlooking the Common and one of the straight macadam paths. During her final illness, she was taken to the Kentish Nursing Home (now Jerningham House) half-way down Mount Sion and next to her old hospital and on the same side, dying in the big room with its own balcony overlooking the garden. For one who had shot up to the very top of the local medical hierarchy almost on arrival, her physical mobility was extremely slow and limited. Unlike my tireless parents, she was no walker, and the only times that she had been to the Spa Hotel and the top of Mount Ephraim was when she had been driven there. As she knew nearly all the doctors in the town, she had little difficulty in getting lifts. My aunt was remarkably good at getting people to do things for her. Two of her Tunbridge Wells friends were even in the habit of taking her with them each year on a September holiday in Menton. Annual trips of this kind were entirely provided for, but she accepted such offerings with an almost regal *hauteur*, as if they had been her due. One felt that she was going out of her way to oblige all those who did her such favours, as if she were doing *them* a favour by being gracious enough to accept them.

It was the same with her nurses; they were always giving her presents – little things to put on the mantelpiece of her sitting-room; and they frequently put in extra hours of duty – all of which she accepted with rather an absent-minded grace.

The 'Maudies' (my father's collective name for Miss Goldeney and Miss Harris – it was the red-haired Miss Harris who was called Maud), who lived together in a large house near the Nevill Tennis Club, although nimble and fast of foot on the tennis courts well into old age, avoided all heights, sticking to the level, from the Pantiles and Chapel Place, to the Nevill Bakery at the far end of the High Street. They never visited my mother; it would have meant going uphill.

Nor would I think of sending any of the double-gin brigade off the Cannon Street train swerving up Grove Hill, in reverse direction to that of the Loves, father and son, as *they* came zig-zagging down. It was the *Common* for them, as they panted and puffed up one of the steepest macadam paths. Baroness Olga (she did not seem to have any other name), the town's only victim of the Russian Revolution, lived in Oblomov-like immobility (not, in fact, prone all day on a sofa, but much of the time seated at the Bridge table) in the trough formed by the bottom end of Madeira Park, lending to an area both dowdy and damp and rather run-down the palely reflected prestige of her Imperial Russian title. The Baroness was pointed out to me once, with awe, by Bobby; she had a high fur collar and a *bandeau*, under a tight-fitting cloche hat, and very long jade ear-rings, and she was smoking a cigarette – in the *street*, indeed in Lower Madeira Park – held in a long black cigarette-holder, like the advertisement for Du Maurier that I used to see in *Punch*. A sledge pulled by little horses would have completed the tableau; but there was no snow on the red and grey brick pavement which was running with water after a sharp shower. Still, we were pretty impressed. She was the first titled person we had ever seen. What is more, she appeared to be rather beautiful, in a sultry sort of way. The Baroness, like

118

the 'Maudies', seemed to have a horror of heights; but it was quite easy for her to stay entirely on the level, reaching the shops by cutting through Cumberland Walk.

Poor Mr Evans – of whose elaborate teas and literary niece I shall speak later – supported on two sticks, and moving forward inch by inch with an agonising slowness and a plucky determination, had a limit of the lower end of Claremont Road and the Grove as far as the entry to Little Mount Sion; it was years since he had been down as far as the shops. I became very fond of Mr Evans; but I used to imitate his difficult progress, taking out a couple of walking-sticks from the stand in the hall of our house and going up and down the long corridor. I did not mean to be cruel, and I knew Mr Evans was in continuous pain, but I still imitated him; my mother would say that it was very wrong thus to make fun of an arthritic old man, and that some day I would be punished for it. But she still laughed at my laboured progress up and down the hall and in and out of her drawing-room.

A schoolboy, following each day a limited choice of fixed itineraries at fixed times, is likely to encounter the same people in the same places at certain times of the day and to acquire a great deal of random information about the likely locations of others. Although I was a regular user of the Common – on my way *to* school (for I could then take in Mr Gripper's tiny sweet-shop just after it had opened) – on my way *from* school, I took another route past the Nursing Homes – I never saw anything shocking take place there: couples the one on the top of the other, in bizarre and fast-accelerating activity, and that sort of thing – probably because it was the wrong time of day and would not be on the morning programme. Not that I was particularly curious about such matters. I was told to avoid the Common on Bank Holidays, so I probably missed the worst.

16 CUTTING CORNERS

The schoolboy, carrying his collective identity card over his left breast (in the rather dreadful form of an embroidered pink rose on a grey background) will be aware that he is himself the object of close observation and that he can be easily picked out as belonging to a given school. There were only two preparatory schools in Tunbridge Wells in the twenties: Rose Hill and Eversley, the former pink and light grey, with pink piping round the edge of the blazer, the latter mauve and dark grey, and with a discreet absence of piping. I was quite happy with the former, though the dreadful piping made me feel that I was giving out a pale pink glow that could be seen in the dark; but one of the Howarth brothers told my sister, at a party, that 'the better sort of people went to Eversley'. At the time, it had seemed quite natural to me that many of my friends should have been the sons of local tradesmen, undertakers and dentists, as well as of officers in the supply services of the Indian Army or in Indian Railways. I was not worried by such distinctions; but my parents were, or at least my mother (prompted no doubt by my aunt, the ultimate authority on the local social nuances) was; and it seemed typical of their embarrassing habit of getting the first foot wrong and of then making matters worse by attempting to retrieve it when it was already too late and the damage had been done, that, at 12 I should have been withdrawn from Rose Hill and sent as a boarder to the Beacon, at Crowborough. The official reason given for the move was that I needed to be taught Greek in preparation for sitting for a scholarship at Shrewsbury – that, at least, is what I was told, in face of my tearful protests, and no doubt that was what Rose Hill was told, too. But, more likely, it was because my mother had become aware of the fact that Rose Hill was 'the wrong type of school'. It was a pity that my parents had not thought of that sooner; they had opted for Rose Hill because it was cheaper than Eversley. They were now sending me to a boarding school which was much more expensive than Eversley and at which I arrived, perched on the folding seat of the Coad Daimler, at 12, three or four years older than the other new boys. It was as if I had been let in surreptitiously through the tradesmen's entrance. It had been the same, several years earlier, with my sister; at first the Girls' High School, right at the top of Grove Hill, had been thought good enough; then at 16, at least two years late, she had been sent as a boarder to the Godolphin. I think even her uniform had been bought second-hand from wherever such things could be obtained (my mother would have known) – possibly, and shamedly, from another Tunbridge Wells parent who had had a daughter there. And when, at the beginning of one term, she had turned up in a new dress, and not in one that had had the collar turned and other adjustments visibly made – my mother was an expert on turning the collars of shirts and blouses and many of my early silk shirts and velvet knickers had been made out of old dresses and odd bits of material – it became a minor sensation throughout the school: 'Diana Cobb has a new dress'. As I was to discover to my own cost, public schoolboys could be as pitilessly observant as public schoolgirls. My parents wanted the best for us both in terms of education and of middle-class priorities. But, by attempting to do things on the cheap, by cutting corners and using back-doors, by giving the appearance of hovering uncertainly over the minutely defined frontiers separating middle class from lower middle class, they had, no doubt quite unwittingly, caused both of us agonies of social embarrassment. Later, I would feel awkward and uneasy when I met my friends from Rose Hill, as though I had done them an injury; and it was worse when they treated me exactly as before. Later still, I attended one or two of their annual Old Boys' Dinners, held in a mock-Tudor establishment at Southborough, and would feel embarrassed by the rather studied heartiness of such occasions. I felt I had moved on from dinners in mock-Tudor restaurants in Southborough.

It was like my father's habit of attending the local meets of the Eridge Hunt on foot and accepting a glass of sherry or of steaming hot punch, or whatever was offered on those freezing occasions by the Huntsman, as if he had been a camp-follower. I felt, when I accompanied him on these outings, that he was being allowed in like a poor relation; he was not even properly dressed, a plus-foured figure on foot in long woollen stockings and stout shoes amidst a sea of mounted pink. Of course, there may not have been any condescension from the horsemen – for some of them knew him at the Tunbridge Wells and Counties Club – but I could still go red with embarrassment, as I looked up, from top-boot level, at the proud riders. Yet there were always plenty more foot-followers who seemed to be perfectly at ease and enjoying themselves on these meets.

For that matter, owing to my mother's insistence that we always spend Christmas dinner with our affluent Sevenoaks cousins, my sister and I were made very much aware that we were *indeed* poor relations – and so we were – and that we were being treated as such. My mother alone seemed thoroughly to enjoy this awful annual ritual. In the end, finding a willing ally in my recently acquired brother-in-law, my father put his foot down, firmly declaring that he would no longer attend these grisly functions; it was one of the few occasions on which he asserted himself and kicked away the extensive local network formed by my mother's sisters.

For many years, too, I had to endure the minor humiliations caused by the habit of another of my aunts – married to one of my medical uncles – of always giving me Christmas and birthday presents that looked as if they had been acquired at jumble sales and Church bazaars and that were *always* of antiquated appearance and design and that generally did not work. I recall, in particular, an awful little black tricycle, made of indestructible iron, its mournful paint flaking with rust, that certainly dated back to the previous reign or even to the one before that. It was not so bad being seen attempting to ride the beastly thing – the rear wheels firmly stuck – in the streets of Portsmouth and Southsea, for nobody knew me there. But I was not going to be seen out with it in Tunbridge Wells. Once back home – the black brute having been transported in the guard's van from Fratton Junction – I took it, on a rainy day, to the top of the Happy Valley and sent it crashing down among the rocks, overhanging evergreens and tall ferns. I climbed down to the bottom; it was still intact and its rear wheels now went round, having come unlocked in the fall. When I returned home without it, my mother made no comment. Even she felt that my aunt Frances – a former nurse from Guy's with a New Zealand accent which might cover up a multitude of social sins (my mother did not have a line on New Zealand accents, but she implied that Frances was common) – pushed economy beyond the bounds of endurance. Her presents were positively insulting; what is more, she would insist on seeing them when she came on one of her (fortunately rare) visits from Berkshire or Waterlooville. I think she enquired about the tricycle; but my mother fobbed her off with some story about it being under repair, how much I missed it, and so on.

Such were the minor agonies brought about by a sudden change of uniform and of collective allegiance, by having to make do with second-best and second-hand, and by having to accept benefits that were not always spontaneously proffered and of which my sister and I would be frequently reminded; apparently, there was an awful lot we should be *grateful* for (including the changes in our education), just as there were always a great many thanking letters to be written. Not that we needed reminding. We wrote them punctually – and hypocriti-cally.

My father seemed to live at several removes from this obsession, with status and appearances; he appeared to be almost unaware of the fragile edifice of middle-class niceties and of the delicate balancing act involved in 'making a little go a long way'. He was a very simple man, as much at ease with the retired railwaymen and artisans whom he met, most after-noons, at the allotments beyond the top of Forest Road, as with his Soudan friends at the club. He would become a different person, less reserved, and reverting to Edwardian jokes and snatches of music-hall songs, once he emerged, in gum-boots, a battered trilby and an old pair of trousers, from the hut in which he kept his gardening tools, as if the hut had been a safe refuge from Tunbridge Wells proprieties. I was often surprised at the warmth with which he was greeted by his fellow-diggers. He had no respect for money as such and was prone to suggest that some of my aunts attached too much importance to appearances. He seemed to be able to live *in* Tunbridge Wells without being part *of* it. His (disastrous) incursion into publishing, in partnership with Eric Partridge, represented no doubt an attempt to escape from it, offering him a pretext to go to London once a week and to Gloucester once or twice a month. But, in this respect, he was quite unlike my mother, my sister, and myself. Until she got married, my sister felt socially insecure, an inhabitant of a sort of class no-man's-land. I sometimes felt something of the sort myself, though my fear of humiliation eased off once I had settled in at Shrewsbury. But, in speaking of my change of blazers and of the rather embattled position we seemed to occupy in social terms, I have wandered far away from the regular – and irregular – itineraries of schoolboys.

17 THE SECRET MAP

Such *regular* itineraries will thus impose at least the outward appearance of good behaviour. For indifferent, or thoroughly *bad* behaviour, the blazer, the round school cap, and the regular itineraries all have to be abandoned. And this is the point at which will come in the tall ferns of the tropical rain-forest, the man-size mauve weeds, the deep hole at the bottom of the ruined garden, the thick and muddy woodlands down towards the brownish, rusty waters of the chalybeate stream, the waist-high weeds surrounding a small, choked-up pond, the giant ferns apparently growing out of the dark rock, an enclosure offering a complete cover, and with a soft floor provided by the thick green and yellow beds of moss, the narrow alley-ways running behind the little houses in Claremont Road, the entries of which it was so easy to miss, the many footpaths connecting one built-up area with another through semi-rural fields, the mysteries of the lower reaches of Upper Grosvenor Road, and even the apparently innocent bluebell and primrose woods. For any schoolboy, when out of school, there are likely to be a great many occasions when it is better not to be seen at all, much less to be recognised.

So, superimposed on the public, respectable map of accountable itineraries there will be another, very private map of the secret places that, remembered or revisited, will still retain a not unexciting odour of sin among the moving, dappled shadows thrown by swaying branches and tall ferns and the noise of insects, under the summer sun: a very personal map of innocence long since lost.

I think that, in most respects, I was much like other schoolboys, timid, in company, about sex, but giving it a great deal of fervid thought, and occasional indulgence, when on my own and unobserved, allowing my imagination briefly to run unclothed and wild, in not very distant mini-jungles within easy walking distance of Tunbridge Wells West, or within hailing distance of the turnstile guarding the official entrance to the High Rocks. Well, I would call them jungles, even when they were bedded with violets and common Kentish wildflowers. I was only mildly depraved, the depravity was mostly in the mind. I had my first sexual experience – warm and agreeable – at the age of 8, while in bed, in the upstairs room facing onto the long narrow garden, in the house in Cumberland Walk, No. 3 or

No. 5. It was unprovoked, and came as a complete surprise; what was agreeable about it was that I now had a secret to share only with myself. With Bobby Atholl and others of my friends, I never touched upon such rich and intimate things. Later, when I was 12, and in my second or third term as a boarder at the Beacon, in Crowborough, I had recently come home for the Easter holidays, and was walking in a field quite near the High Woods and just off the deep-banked road to Kippings Cross; it was a sunny afternoon, and I was thinking about nothing in particular, when I felt a sudden, enveloping warmth inside me. I was *in love*, with a boy at the school called Hook. It was a delicious, exciting, enriching, almost holy feeling that I carried round with me like a secret jewel concealed from sight, to be briefly taken out and admired when I was alone and unobserved, giving to my room at home the excitement of a treasure-house. I thought a great deal about Hook for the rest of the holidays. But, of course, back at school, I never gave him, or anyone else, a hint of my feelings. I did not want the cruel wind of reality to come and blow down my private palace of cards. No one would know – least of all my parents – how *rich* I had all at once become.

Others followed at Shrewsbury – boys eyed and admired (and even photographed) – from afar. At least affairs so one-sided offered one advantage: they could not lead to disappointment, despair, deprivation, jealousy. As they had never begun, so they could not end, only gradually fade away to be replaced by others. A combination of imagination – unrestrained and constantly fuelled – and timidity thus enabled me to cocoon myself in a series of loves (only one at a time) that were little more than self-indulgent fantasies, though there would be a sharp extra shock of private pleasure if I heard that the current object of my unspoken and unsuspected inclinations was showing quite concrete favours to X or to Y, or, better still, to both X and Y. Hook had been different, an object of perfection, almost removed from any physical dimension. Now

I liked to imagine – better, to have pretty strong evidence – that the latest object of my admiration was in fact quite depraved, or well on the way to becoming so. I would follow his steady downward slope and his steadily improving form from not very far away – the width of a corridor, the length of a passage – and with the excitement of the revelation, clearer and clearer, of an apparently insatiable perversity; nor did I grudge in the least the pleasure, often noisily acknowledged by the most recent recipient of such favours, apparently to be obtained from intimate contact with such budding professionalism. One of those thus favoured – a rather simple, straightforward boy, whom I liked – and still hot from a shared bed in which he had been discovered by Authority, even came to tell me, in detail, about his good fortune, which now looked like turning into a misfortune, while still under the full shock of discovery. He sat on my bed, in such a state of agitation, that the bed trembled under him, while he gave me an account of the discovery. I did my best to reassure him, saying that I did not think Authority would report the incident. I felt myself divided between hilarity and vicarious interest, for it was now clear to me that the enthusiastic young performer had completed the tour of his bedroom. He was certainly doing wonders and seemed to be heading either for a brilliant future or for sudden disaster. It was pretty much of a dead-end, though, as far as I was concerned. I think I preferred it that way. I could fill in what was missing-and there was not very much of that, such was the increasingly brazen flaunting of his depravity – for myself. In due course – as is no doubt the case with so many public schoolboys – my sexual inclinations took a more orthodox direction, first of all under the guidance of the professional expertise of the rue de la Lune in the *dixième*, though they long remained highly romantic, positively courting the difficulties imposed by place, distance, exoticism, and circumstance. My Shrewsbury fantasies – because they were fantasies (though attached to individuals of flesh and blood) – left no cherished

association with *place*, no recollection of a stunted tree, or of a
deep bank falling down to the level of the curving river, of a
distant line of blue hills, leaving no map of love, no *Carte du
Tendre*, to which to return, as a nostalgic visitor, years later. In
terms of sexual experience, Shrewsbury had provided me with
the same sort of vicarious enjoyment as, many years later, I
would derive from reading – and re-reading – *Les Liaisons
Dangereuses*. Mentally, I had been both Madame de Merteuil
and Valmont, as I followed the fortunes of one who had shown
early signs of promise and who had proceeded, in a very short
space, to fulfil them beyond the bounds of even the most
sanguine expectations. No pupil of mine, it is true; but I had
spotted the hidden signs of virtuosity from the moment I had
first set eyes on him. It gave me a proprietary, as well as an
erotic, interest in his career.

In Tunbridge Wells, the secret map was, for quite a long
time, a solitary one, that I walked or cycled alone, though, in
the end, this indigence was remedied, giving the place a new
dimension and a whole series of new itineraries – or, rather, old
ones, refurbished, a secret *shared*, placed over an older, lonely
map composed of dreams and make-believe. But that is quite
another story, and another Tunbridge Wells, thirty or forty
years on; and I am straying far away from childhood and
adolescence and from the sudden wonderful awareness of the
innocent and unknowing Hook, as I sat on a stile overlooking a
field and a country road beneath a high bank covered in violets,
near the High Woods, at the age of 12.

18 THE KRUGER SOVEREIGN

In respect of villainy and destructiveness, I was *more* like other
schoolboys, less private, less secretive, more participant than in
the enervating and closely guarded intimacies of love and sex. If
I wished to shoot at moving targets with my airgun (a gift of

very trusting parents), I would not choose the High Street or Mount Ephraim – though, in the course of one foolhardy operation, I fired at a green Autocar bus (I was a partisan of the rival company Redcar) outside the Central Station, the pellet fortunately bouncing off the rounded rear of the vehicle unseen save by myself. I also put a neat round hole through an upper window of a neighbouring house in Claremont Road, an enterprise in which I was detected. My father had to go round and apologise; my patents were not unduly cross, putting it down to 'high spirits', which they must have preferred to low ones. I sought out a new housing estate, the houses completed and awaiting a few fittings and then occupation, and with many inviting, unwatched and unwatchful windows, the glass of each one with a round white blob painted in the middle, like a target, as though especially for my benefit, after the men had left work and the place seemed completely deserted.

Ringing doorbells, then running away, would take me to areas previously unvisited (and, later, prudently avoided, so that the doorbell map would be a constantly expanding one, taking me further and further out). But it was a poor sort of sport. I preferred the allurements of gardens gone wild and sad, roofless houses awaiting demolition. There was one such huge garden, its box-hedges still surviving beside the broken walls and foundations of a large ruined house, at the top end of Nevill Park, the red, purple, and mauve-flowering weeds growing taller than my height at 12, the headless statue of a nude boy picking a thorn out of his foot lying toppled in long grass at some distance away from its broken plinth, a decaying summer-house in rotting and collapsing thatch at the end of one of the still just visible grassy alleys. Better still, one huge grey façade, with a pillared entrance in the middle, like a stage set or the remains of a barracks burnt down in Co. Wicklow during the Troubles, discoverable if one pushed through a piece of broken fencing next to the big Methodist church off Mount Ephraim and standing in black silhouette against the sinking sun, down a steep slope cut like a battlefield, with deep trenches and bits of masonry, and fallen chimney-pots. Thirty yards beyond the black façade, there was an enormous hole in the ground, the bottom of which, quite dark even at midday, was approachable down a precipitous winding path that one could negotiate by holding onto the long roots that stuck out from the yellow clay; at the bottom, there was a small area of brown, brackish water; a boy's paradise, the discovery of which I regarded as an enrichment to my life of adventure. I kept the secret of the Hole to myself. But someone else must have stumbled upon it, because, on my next visit, I found that it had been covered over with planks and netting. Apparently, there had been an accident; a boy from King Charles choir school had been severely hurt. This wild paradise was all that was left of a large estate and a Georgian house, the site that had been set aside for the new hospital.

In the twenties Tunbridge Wells, though a small town in terms of population – 20,000, perhaps a bit more – was extending rapidly; and already a number of such vast old grey stone houses, hidden in the remains of heavily-treed gardens, even parks, were awaiting demolition or were already half-demolished, their roofs half off, the rafters showing, the slates scattered among the dead leaves, to make way for new estates and for muddy, unmade streets of undistinguished jerry-built houses. The intermediary stage – the demolition half-done, the ground not yet cleared – was the ideal time to move in, even if it meant making a hole in a fence, tearing down a plank or two (it generally did, and this would provide a tasty hors-d'oeuvre to the greater possibilities of destruction that must surely lie beyond). In retrospect, I have the impression that the twenties were a golden age for this sort of thing, the post-War building boom offering a wonderful stimulus to long-drawn-out demolitions, most of them carried out by hand, as if especially to oblige those in my age-group who were good at climbing, were not afraid of barbed wire, were unconcerned (at the time at least, it would be different when one got back home) about torn clothing, cuts, scratches and bruises, and for whom the sight of a stout tall fence, recently erected, was both a challenge and a promise of the hidden pleasures on the other side. I had an eye for those fences, as I roamed, generally alone, the more promising outskirts of the town, the dank lower-reaches of that mysterious, nameless zone that could be described as 'behind Mount Ephraim'. Some of these I would mentally note down for my solitary future enjoyment; some – the more stupendous: several acres of ruin and semi-ruin, numerous out-houses, stables, rotting verandahs, rotting summer-houses, rusting iron balconies, a really big job in prospect – I would indicate to one or two friends and accomplices, so that we could return, capless and blazerless, and, as we imagined, difficult to identify: long grey stockings, unpolished black shoes covered in green mould from close encounters with rotting, damp wood, grey flannel shirts – pink ties hidden away in pockets – and shorts in the same material, green and yellow in the seat, indicating a recent escapade: the standard *cap-à-pied* equipment of the schoolboy released from school and divested of compromising heraldic symbols and well-known combinations of colours – the whole surmounted by a variety of countenances: freckled, pink, pallid, sallow, purple: of eyes in different colours.; of noses mostly up-lifting and runny, and hair: straight, standing on end (as mine did, obstinately, in a whitish tuft at the crown), curly, tousled, spiky, and generally unbrushed.

On most of these expeditions – so far as I recall – we remained undetected and undisturbed. Had we been discovered, we would no doubt have argued – though I do not know with what success – that we were co-operating in the process of demolition, were indeed one or two steps ahead of those who had been officially entrusted with the job, thus relieving them, in advance, of some of the work. But one of my single-handed operations did end in disaster. On returning from school on a warm spring evening, I had taken my airgun and rushed down

Claremont Road to the sharp bend at the level of Miss Fleetwood's house, and below which stood a row of a dozen new houses, just completed. I had watched the progress of the building with attention and had realised that this was my last chance – or almost my last chance – before residents actually started moving in. I began on the house nearest to Claremont Road: first the front, then the back – there was a small glazed window on that side, no doubt a lavatory, that splintered most excitingly from the small round hole into a spreading cobweb. I moved on to the next house down – front and back, leaving the glazed window to the last; this time, it shattered, with a loud report. And so on, front and back, down the unmade street, glazed windows splintering with a lot of noise. I had just picked off the round white blob of my twenty-seventh window front – there were only eleven more left – when I felt a tightening at the back of my neck, the pressure increasing so that I was unable to turn round. A rough voice from behind, and very high up, said: 'Caught you in the act, my lad. Your father will hear about this', adding that he had been watching me as I had proceeded along the road from No. 1 to No. 27. He then came in front of me, standing over me so that I was in shadow and could not see him properly, seizing me by the lobe of my left ear, pulling on it very hard, as if it had been a door-bell, and taking my airgun with his other hand. His face was in silhouette, so I could not make out the expression, but I found my nose close up to a waistcoat and the lapels of a shabby, shiny blue suit, and took in a powerful whiff of sweat. He was, he said, a builder's foreman, his job to keep an eye on the houses after the men had gone home; and he was going, he added sickeningly, to take me, there and then, to my father's, so as to tell him what I had been up to, *and* a Rose Hill boy at that! (I had been in too much of a hurry to remove the accursed blazer.) Although absolutely terrified by the realisation of the enormity of my crime, and very near to tears, both from the pain and as a result of the disastrous turn taken by what should have been a supremely satisfying outing, I still had enough presence of mind to realise that he probably did not know where my parents lived. We started walking, side by side, and though I was the one being led – by the ear – when we reached Claremont Road, I turned towards the left, and thus, ear in hand, we headed towards the Grove, and away from my father's house. On the way, he asked me my name. I said it was Featherstone or something of that sort; and he did not question me further on that score. So I realised – with immense relief – that he would not be able to find out where my father lived. When we reached the Grove, which was quite empty – it was getting late, and I had taken quite a long time over my twenty-seven windows, wanting to savour each one, and keeping the glazed ones to the last – he all at once changed his tack. If I did not pay for the damage, he said, he would haul me off to the Police Station. But he would give me to the next day to raise the money: £4. He would meet me at the Grove, by the swings, at 5, and if I produced the money, he would not do anything more about it. But if I failed to do so, it would be the police. And, at this point, he let go of my ear, looked me in the face – he had blue eyes and was bald, and I noticed that he wore a shirt that did not have a collar – gave my other ear a parting tweak, and walked off with a shuffling gait. I stayed in the Grove long enough to see him cut down the little street that led to the High Street at the level of W. H. Smith; and, once I was sure he was not watching, rather than make my way *up* Claremont Road, past the fatal site, I decided to play safe by approaching my home from behind, through Birdcage Walk. I spent some time making sure that Claremont Road was clear, rushed up the steps, my head well down, and let myself in furtively. By a stroke of luck, my father was at his club, my mother out at Bridge. I shut myself in my room and thought out a plan of action. I *had* to find the £4, there was no doubt in my mind about that. It did not occur to me that the collarless man had no means of tracking me down if I failed to turn up at the 5 pm rendezvous the next day; nor did it occur to me that the

man, who looked rather shabby, and had not insisted on taking
me to the police rightaway, might not be a builder's foreman.
For, if he *had* been, would he have stood by passively watching,
while I knocked off my twenty-seven windows? Would he not
have intervened much sooner in order to prevent further
damage? But such questions did not occur to me at the time. I
was still too terrified to think clearly. I had been quite clever in
concealing my address and in leading him away towards the
Grove. But, so I thought, Tunbridge Wells was a small place,
he knew my school, he would be sure to find me in the end.
Better pay him; it was the only way out.

In an old medicine-chest that stood on castors, in my room (it
had been abandoned by the previous tenant), I kept a number
of my treasures: a china puddle-duck with a broken beak, a
celluloid pig, what passed for an Ancient Egyptian necklace
(bought at a CMS fête in Crowborough), a box of water-colour
paints, a child's miniature cooking set, several billion German
marks in notes, a cigar-box full of funny-shaped coins with
holes through their middle and Arab symbols on them, several
George III pennies, a George IV half-crown, a William & Mary
sixpence, a Charles II twopenny piece, and, of untold value,
the pride of my collection, three handsome Kruger sovereigns,
bearing the bearded profile of the old President, and given to
me by my parents (my father had been in the Boer War, and
had met my mother shortly after the Peace, in Bloemfontein). I
put two of the sovereigns in my pocket, wrapping them in
rather a dirty handkerchief, so that they would not clink – even
so, I could feel the weight of them, like a weight of guilt, getting
heavier every minute, and burning through my shorts, as if
actually exposed to my thigh – when my parents came back, and
I had to struggle – as if unconcerned – through my supper. I
was sure that they would be able to see through the grey flannel.
But I got through the rest of the evening without mishap; and it
was only when I was getting into bed that I remembered that
the man had gone off with my airgun and that I would have to

account for that. Yet another problem. In my agitation, I had not even noticed its absence.

The next day I spent an uneasy time at school in the weighty company of the pair of Presidents; after school, I went to Payne's, the silversmith's in the High Street, standing outside till I was sure the shop was empty of customers (I had put my cap, tie and blazer in a bag that I generally used for my swimming things and that I had taken off with me, for this purpose in mind, in the morning; if my mother had asked about it, I would have said that we were having an extra visit to the Public Baths, it was a risk worth taking; but she had not noticed it), then, going in, I handed over one Kruger sovereign, saying I wanted to sell it in order to help me towards buying a new bicycle. The man looked at it through a magnifying-glass screwed into his eye, weighed it on tiny golden scales, and then said he'd give me £5 for it. I accepted at once, desperate to be out of the shop before anyone else came in – it was the sort of place some of my mother's friends regularly patronised – shot out of the door, then slowed down and walked with what I hoped looked like nonchalance, towards the Grove. I did not have to wait long. The man turned up, just after 5, holding my airgun under his arm, from the direction of Little Mount Sion. This time he did not take me by the ear, merely asking: 'Do you have the money?' When I said I had, he looked almost pleased. I. handed him the four notes and he gave me back my airgun and went off, this time towards Meadow Hill Road, as if he were going to the Station. I waited till he had left the Grove then headed for home. I had somehow to reach my room without being seen, for it would have been hard to explain what I had been doing with my airgun at school. I reckoned that mother would be sitting at her desk in the drawing-room, doing her accounts. I reached my room safely, put the airgun down, and slipped, the second Kruger sovereign back in its drawer, with its remaining companion. The £1 I hid in the fire-place, on a sort of shelf a little up the chimney. I spent it later in the summer at Shorncliffe, where I was staying with the son of the Deputy-Chaplain-General to the Army. After hearing his father preach a vigorous sermon at the well-attended garrison church, and having Sunday lunch, my friend took me into Folkestone, where we bought several packets of Gold Flake and two large bottles of beer; my friend seemed used to both, but smoking and drinking what remained of my Kruger sovereign made me violently sick; perhaps it was a punishment. So, for the moment, I had made it. I opened the drawing room door; my mother looked up from her little red account book and asked me if I'd had a good day. I said that I had, and, in a way, I had had.

That was not quite the end of it. Some time later, while checking through my room, my mother discovered that one of the Krugers was missing. I was closely questioned, and lied steadfastly: I did not know anything about it, could not *think* what had happened to it. We had a temporary maid at the time, a young girl. I think my mother suspected her, for I heard my parents discussing the loss; and she went not long after, though I gathered from one or two prudent and oblique questions put to my mother, she got another, permanent job. I kept quiet, and felt wretched. But what could I have done? I gave the building site a wide berth. But I suppose the windows were replaced. I never saw the man again, but, for some weeks, I avoided the Grove. All in all, I had been pretty lucky. I kept the other two Krugers; and when I was in the Army and stationed in Cardiff, I put them regularly in pawn, in the pawnshops in West Bute Street, in Tiger Bay, to get me through from Monday to Friday pay day. I think, in the end, they had to remain in pawn, because I did not have enough to retrieve them; but whether this happened while I was still in Tiger Bay or at a later stage of the War, I cannot remember. Later, in Paris, my silver cigarette case, a twenty-first birthday present from my uncle, and inscribed in my name, ended up in the *Mont de Piété*, opposite the Archives, my grandfather's gold whole-hunter went a different way; I had to leave it with a restaurant proprietor, to pay the backlog of the dinners I had already eaten at his establishment. In retrospect, I think I had been lucky in my choice of Payne's, a firm that had long been used to customers from the Empire. They had probably seen plenty of Kruger sovereigns come their way and would not have seen anything odd in the fact of one being brought in by an >untidy boy of eleven.

19 THE SHIP

A concluding note to these evocations could be provided by the surprising view offered both from the rough football pitch that stood high above the London Road on the Common side, and from the seats on the upper paths as they climbed towards Gibraltar House, built into its rock, and the top of Mount Ephraim – the seats occupied at 6.50 or so by the washed-up bowler-hatted debris of the City: at first glance, a conventional urban scene: the red brick eighteenth-century doctor's house, with its wrought-iron early-Victorian green balconies and canopies, the small, cream-coloured shop of Romary's Water Biscuits, bearing the royal arms in gold, the ugly red Homoeopathic Hospital, the Ladies' Bridge Club in white, with white wooden balconies and steps covered by a wooden filigree canopy, the early-nineteenth century grey building that housed Rose Hill School. It was from the windows of the school, on a hot and sunny day in 1927 or 1928 that, having left our desks, we had stared down eagerly onto the London Road, as crowds gathered on the grass that separated the road from the path that went past the private hotels, as well as on the football pitch high above the road on the other side; there was an air of expectancy as well as of festivity, as the crowds steadily thickened, to line both sides of the road continuously and, as the traffic in the direction of the Pantiles and the Coast thinned out, then ceased altogether, till the road was quite empty, just a glistening black stream, as if it too were waiting for something. People on our side of the road kept looking to the right, and those on the far side craned their necks leftwards, both groups gradually falling into almost complete silence. Then we could hear faint cheers coming from the top of the road, the volume of noise growing rapidly, as it ran downhill in our direction. Now we could just see three cars, travelling rather slowly: first, a very tall closed Daimler – the bottom part of a chauffeur's uniform and three pairs of striped trousers from the knee downward, spats and black shoes just visible inside – then an open car, painted green, then another tall closed Daimler, with more knees and striped legs and spats and black shoes. It was the green car that had been the cause of all the excitement: alone, in the back, sitting bolt upright, and looking straight ahead, was a very handsome man with wavy fair hair and dressed in a light grey suit. He looked bored, and seemed unaware of the cheers and the clapping and of the waving of the little flags and white handkerchiefs, as if only concerned to get wherever he was going, his well-shaped head fixed in a forward position; though quite close, he appeared remote and preoccupied, and very stiff. Then the big green car disappeared round the corner, followed closely by the second Daimler, and the crowds started moving away, while the normal summer traffic reappeared, as it headed for the sea. We went back to our desks. I don't know how the others felt, but I was vaguely disappointed: it had been my first view of royalty, and I had expected something more dramatic, a central figure more participant, less bored; it was the only time I ever saw the Prince of Wales.

Beyond the school, lower down the path, stood a row of private hotels in red brick, their names in gold letters, some of the letters missing. In front of one of the hotels, there was a mock-Gothic gate house. But, behind the tall Rose Hill building, and partly hidden by it, the masts, derricks, bridge, superstructure, wheel-house, the big red funnel circled in black, white railings, four lifeboats attached to their hoists, and three lines of port-holes, there stood out boldly a full-sized merchant ship, black, with a white surround, and a waterline just visible in red, very spick and span, its paint gleaming even on dull days. On certain days-generally at the week-end – there would be complicated signals, in four lines of little flags, flying merrily from the fore-mast, spelling out their coded coloured messages. The ship could be spotted from the football pitch, and further up. And even from Mount Ephraim, the top of the funnel, the masts and the derricks could still be made out, as they peeped between the elms of Rose Hill garden. I don't know what visitors can have made of the land-locked ship harbouring in this riverless town, well over twenty miles from the sea, and which, seen close to, could be observed to be floating in grass up to its so-called waterline, but residents were rather proud of it, as one might be of a shared joke or of being in the secret. Its presence seemed to add to the singularity of the place; and there could be no harm in that, for Tunbridge Wells was not like other places, above all not the least bit like the wretched Tonbridge (Tunbridge Wells prided itself on its 'u', and there could have been no worse sin than to have spelt it wrong). Rudyard Kipling might have the top half of a battleship, embedded in concrete, in his garden at Burwash; d'Annunzio, his fellow-fraud, could have an aeroplane hanging from the ceiling of his dining-room, and the bridge of a cruiser sunk into his lawn, *we* had a merchant vessel, with a scrubbed deck and coiled ropes laid out in neat patterns, a bridge, a compass, a sextant, speaking-tubes, a wheel-house, two fog-horns, charts in little pigeon-holes, port and starboard lights, three decks, a hold, living-quarters, hatches, winches, all in the garden of a preparatory school. In 1942 two Polish airmen, who were then my pupils, came to Tunbridge Wells. After spending an evening in the Compasses and elsewhere, it became clear that they would not be able to make it back to London that night, so

I walked them to the ship, approaching it from the hidden starboard side, took them on board up the wooden steps, and laid them out on some mattresses below deck – I could not find where the hammocks were stored, which was just as well for, even assuming that I could have got them into them, and they were pretty big men, they would soon have fallen out of them. I left them snoring heavily. But when I came for them in the morning, they told me that they had woken up in a state of considerable confusion, wondering where they were, what they were doing on a ship when they had had no recollection of having been anywhere near the harbour, what a merchant ship was doing in the middle of a lawn, and what was it for, in any case, as it did not move and had no engines. I wanted them to come back again to Tunbridge Wells; I would show them a bit more of the place, but my two Polish stowaways never did.

20 PICTURES

It was a large, double-fronted shop about halfway down the fashionable side of the High Street. The fashionable side was on the north side. It was on the north side that my mother met her friends, ladies in sensible hats, tweed suits, Jaeger jerseys, baskets, and heavy shoes, with dogs on leads, and stopped at a series of gossiping-posts, a dozen or more: the Nevill Bakery, the better chemist, Payne's, the silversmith, Goulden & Curry, the coffee-shop which also sold expensive chocolates, and smelt of both, the butcher's, a dress-shop, and, at the far end, a bank, while I dragged behind, pretending to be engrossed in a window, or walked ahead, looking back, as I hoped, reproachfully and eloquently as my mother progressed slowly from dog-accompanied female couple to dog-accompanied female couple. Anything to avoid all the ritual questions: 'How are you enjoying school? What are you doing in the holidays? How nice for your mother to have you at home!'

Pictures

The north side, raised up high above road level in four or five steps to the brick pavement, was always a long drag, my mother's shopping-basket offering little more than a pretext for the conversational halts between ten and eleven. Perhaps the south side was unfashionable because it was so much lower, though it did include the best cutler's in town – a small, very neat shop, kept and owned by a school-friend of mine, a pink-faced man with watery blue eyes, who, surprisingly, had not lost trade during the war though he had been a Conscientious Objector. I admired him for his nerve, though it did seem rather strange to have been a pacifist within that well-stocked little arsenal of shining and lethal-looking knives. Also on the south side was Mr Edwards' prestigious sports shop. Mr Edwards was a stunningly good-looking Welshman who had lost all trace of a Welsh accent and who had the conventional upper-class features of an English army officer. Mr Edwards looked like, and spoke like, a gentleman; but he wasn't one. However, he was very much in demand as a tennis coach even with mothers of young girls. He had a tanned complexion, a fine head of white hair and well-formed features. He seemed incongruous standing behind the counter in his own shop; indeed, he was not *quite* a shopkeeper, certainly not *just* a shopkeeper. One felt that his right place was all in impeccable white, doing beautiful strokes, on one of the knockabout courts at the Nevill Tennis Club. Mr Edwards was something of a social phenomenon. Even in his shop, he wore a blazer, as if he were just looking in between two games, so that one felt rather apologetic about catching him on the wing and keeping him from playing for Kent or Sussex, or both. It was said that he had a wife, but she was kept hidden away somewhere. Perhaps she was common. So Mr Edwards gave the appearance of being a free man, *l'homme disponible*, ever ready to step into the breach, and make up a fourth in mixed-doubles. There were rumours that he was generally *disponible* for other games as well, though my mother would have dismissed such talk as uncharitable. Though I must have known him for some twenty years, my memory of him is that he was ageless, a handsome man fixed somewhere in the middle of the thirties. I associate him with spring and high summer, though his shop must have remained open in the winter too. Yet I cannot picture him out of his white shirt and blazer. Perhaps he was indeed a transient resident, spending the winter coaching in South Africa or on the Riviera. Certainly he always emerged from the very worst winters as beautifully tanned as ever. He was as discreet as he was naturally polite, in an easy, confident way. It is quite possible that he was indeed everything that he looked: a fine-featured, loose-limbed creature of the sun, with a slow-swinging, powerful and deep back-hand, and a series of perfect cricket strokes. He also taught golf, and gave driving lessons. Yet, somehow, he did seem almost too good to be true. I don't remember him leaving the place. It was just that, some time after the War, he was not there any more, as if he had been unable to step out of the thirties. The shop and the name remained, but no Mr Edwards. It would have been too shocking to have seen him getting old and decrepit.

Half-way along the fashionable side was the big picture-shop. I suppose the pictures were changed from time to time; some may even have been sold. But the display seems to have had a solid, residual invariability: in the place of honour, the Young Crusader kneeling before a not overladen altar (an Anglican one, of course) in the uniform of a young subaltern of the First World War, a shaft of sunshine catching the sheen of his fair hair and of his naked sword. The poor fellow hung there all through the thirties. I could see why no one would buy him. The War was something that had to be discreetly veiled in a place like Tunbridge Wells. I found the invariable presence of the Young Crusader offensive and quite out of character with a place in which no one died young. I wished the Almighty would take against him, switch off the perfectly-aimed shaft of sunlight. He was still there – a military Peter Pan, more than twenty years out of date – in September 1939. By then, he had outlasted the Tree Cathedral, a grove of tall elms in autumn, the ground strewn with fallen leaves, and a shaft of sunlight shining through the centre of the grove to pick out the reds, browns, yellows and greens of the thick carpet of the ground. The Tree Cathedral was replaced by another one, this time of oaks, and in high summer, the shaft of sunlight turned on at a different angle. Snipe Flying over a Norfolk Broad ran for about five years, when it acquired a sticker marked SOLD in red. Bluebell Woods lasted out the whole of the thirties and the entire War. Stage Coaches drew up at Merry Snow-Covered Posting-Houses: no takers. Cornish fishing ports with cobbled streets running down to the gaily coloured boats in the little sunlit harbour; they would still be there in the invariable November or February fog that would hang over the High Street. The middle classes failed to respond. I did see people go into the shop, but only to get their own pictures framed.

Most people would not have needed to buy reproductions, in any case. The many Tunbridge Wells drawing-rooms I entered had their walls crammed with landscapes in water-colours dating back to the beginning of the century, and signed, in rather elaborate initials in sepia or dark brown. Indeed, most of these drawing-rooms had a light, chintzy, feminine quality, a predominance of pinks and old rose, cream and pale green; and, because I found feminine company much more reassuring than that of grown men, I could appreciate the feminine ambience of these pretty rooms decorated with vases of sweet peas, and would be hardly aware of the absence of a male presence. Indeed, many of these drawing-rooms would be shared by *two* women, the water-colours, in contrasting styles, signalling two sets of initials, the walls having been allocated to each, as the result of some private treaty.

Most of these water-colours were amateur works of some skill and pale charm. Some of them represented a muted, curiously English-looking Holy Land, an East Anglian Bethlehem, a

Dead Sea that might have been a Norfolk Broad, a Lahore or a Bombay that lay soothingly under a Suffolk sky and beneath a gentle sun. At my prep school – the Beacon, not Rose Hill, I had been the runner-up for the Divinity Prize, a bitter disappointment, for the winner got a water-colour painted by the rather churchy father of the headmaster's wife ('Mrs Sir'), depicting the Sea of Galilee, which had the gentle shades of the Stour Estuary. The Apostles, it was evident, from the picture I had longed for, and had so narrowedly failed to get, were East Anglians, the sort of ruddy people that one saw on the red-sailed barges of the Colne. I liked the Bible Story to be in gentle English colours, and my favourite picture in the High Street depicted a fresh-faced Jesus Christ, with long, well-combed chestnut hair and wearing a loose-fitting pale pink robe and modern-looking sandals, standing under a palm tree in light green, with little children: blonde and pink, a lightish yellow, an apologetic, watery black, with black faces that showed no trace of negroid features, and looking up at him, as he managed to stroke their raised heads collectively. The little one in rather unconvincing, watered-down black did not have very much on, just a pink cloth round his middle, but enough to be decent; unlike Jesus, all the children were bare-foot, but as they were sitting in the sand, as on the beach at Frinton or Tankerton, this was quite easy to explain; they would have left their shoes in lockers before coming down to the beach. The picture might have been a group portrait of those who were no doubt the particular concern of my father, as secretary of the local branch of the CMS, though none of the children looked a least bit like his description of the Fuzzy-Wuzzies of the South Soudan, of whom he had been especially fond, and to whom he had been in the habit of preaching when he had been down there. This gentle, reassuring picture was in Christ Church, not far from the Nevill Bakery and the Hole in the Wall.

Even my mother, a water-colourist of more than average skill – she had taught water-colours and drawing, as well as maths to the Boer girls of the Eunice High School, Bloemfontein – could make the sand and scrub and the blazing sky of the South Soudan as gentle on the eye as the beach at Pevensey, and the distant blue mountains as soft as the Welsh Hills. A street in Omdurman had houses of unmistakable Arab design, but the sky was a very pale blue with fleecy scudding clouds. A dirt track tapering away towards the line of the Drakensbergs looked as if it might have been at home in my mother's native Berkshire, rather than in the harsh glare of the Free State. When I first went to the Transvaal, I was amazed by the implacability of the light. My mother's water-colours had given no hint of anything so brutal. Perhaps water-colour was just not right for Africa.

But most such water-colours were of very English gardens, of herbaceous borders and rockeries, of large houses in pale pink brick set in smudgy, fluffy trees, of Gothic walls in timid grey with delicate red poppies growing out of them, of gentle ploughed fields in light beige. The spacious houses and walled gardens depicted childhood homes, when the artists had been girls in their teens, in the utter safety and stillness of pre-War years; and so, often, they were sad, timid monuments to better things, slightly pathetic and incongruous – like Miss Fleet-wood's little Cromwellian museum in her tiny front-room – in the cramped little drawing-rooms, the tatters of an impoverished gentility.

I speak of water-colours as if they were already relics of the past, even modest family heirlooms, in the twenties and thirties. There were in fact still plenty of practitioners – more often female than male, the former in white cotton hats, the latter in panamas and alpaca jackets – during my childhood, and, on fine days, one would see easels up all over the Common, the Wellington Rocks, the Toad Rock, Crowborough Beacon and the Happy Valley providing the favourite subjects, with Gibraltar House, the Mount Edgcumbe Hotel, and the skyline of the town, with the tower of Holy Trinity and the green dome

of the Opera House offering a centre, running them close.
People with easels and folding chairs were taken as much for
granted as even more encumbered fishermen would be today,
so that, when I first went to Paris in 1935, I felt no nervousness
when sitting with my sketching-pad in the rue Galande, or on a
seat on the Pont des Arts, facing the Vert Galant. People took
me for granted, glanced at my pad, and passed on.

For such enthusiasts, there was a little shop – Saltmarsh –
that sold easels, Winsor & Newton sketching-pads, paint-
boxes, tubes of paint, and the marvellous L & C Hartmudt
yellow pencils, all the way from BB, through common-or-
garden HB, to sharp, fierce H, the product of Czechoslovakia,
in Vale Road, not far from the courtyard of the Central Station.
Pencil-drawing, as much as pen-and-ink – and much more
difficult than pen-and-ink (that is why I stuck mostly to the
latter) had survived well into the thirties, both at schools, and in
later life, among amateurs, as well as professionals like George
Belcher, a man with a beautiful and deceptively unstudied
pencil line. This attractive skill helped to lend the thirties the
delicate shades and modest half-tones of an infinite range of
blacks and greys. Pencils and pencil-boxes had survived and
continued to flourish as much as water-colour paint-boxes in
various sizes. There was a local artist with a very pretty line who
did pencil drawings of oast-houses and long black Kentish
barns, country churches, fishing boats and barges, clapboard
cottages (absolutely made for the pencil, with their clear
horizontal lines), ivy-covered ruins (plenty of work for the BB
here, especially in the vigorous cross-hatching of the jagged
holes and dark recesses of the stonework), moated granges,
ruined windmills, hulks lying blackly in the mud of the
Medway Estuary, wooden fisherman's huts on the shore at
Hastings, old railway cuttings, the dried beds of half-built
canals that had started in all good faith and that had petered out
wretchedly after a painful mile or two. These were to illustrate
the books that he wrote: *Unknown Kent* and *A Detective in*

Sussex. Kent especially, being so much in wood, made admirable pencil country, though I think Essex would have made an even better one. The pencil was the ideal instrument of the walking observer in plus-fours as he stalked a derelict oast-house, with its wooden ribs revealed, or a semi-ruined wooden cottage. The lovely yellow Hartmudt pencils linger on for me as the emblems of a still reassuring thirties. Appropriately, they started to disappear in the early forties, never re-emerging. Perhaps they were minor victims of the cataclysm let loose by the folly and the fanaticism of Hitler. For the pencil could never be corrosive, could never bite like an etching or a pen-and-ink. It was the humble, gentle tool of the eye for the everyday and the banal, of picturesque decay, rather than of horrible putrefaction. I expect pencils are still made in Czechoslovakia, as they certainly are in Boulogne-sur-Mer, but the famous firm has disappeared without a trace. And the Age of the Pencil, one of middle-class amateurism and relative innocence, has passed away.

21 TEA AT MR EVANS'S

I don't know actually *how* it started, for, later on, it seemed as if we had always known him, he became so much part of our familiar topography, so that each time we went past no. 69, on the way to the Grove or to the shops, we would think of him and wonder what he'd be doing in the big grey house with the impressive entry that jutted out, like an extra room, into the curving drive, at that time of the morning, for he was never seen outside in the road before 2. Nor did I ever discover what he did in the evening, save the fact that he never went out after dark. But there must have *been* a beginning, just as much as, sadly, there was to be an end. In retrospect, I think it must have been the tie that brought about the first, tentative move; my mother would know about ties, it was just the sort of thing that she

147

spotted, and it would not have been the first time that she had seen one in chocolate, blue and gold; there had been our stay at a big hotel in St Leonard's, a wonderful week in February when I was 8 or 9, and the doctor had recommended the sea air as the best thing for my bronchitis. There had been a chocolate, blue and gold in discreet evidence in the enormous and elaborate chintzed drawing-room when we had been listening to the news: further down, a brown sports-coat, a beige pull-over, and plus-fours of the oatmeal colour that my father used to favour, the whole ending in heavy walking-shoes: a very polite and considerate old man who had talked to me as if I had been a grown-up. My father and my sister had not been on that trip, so it must have been my mother who made the first approach to another middle-aged gentleman in an old Salopian tie. I suppose she just stopped and talked to him one day when he was taking his slow and painful exercise in Claremont Road. He would have been trapped, leaning on his two sticks and unable to beat a retreat. My mother would have been on her way to Bridge at the Widows' Flats, 'I see you are a Salopian, my son is going to that school'. That's how it would have been.

Well, Mr Evans *was*. But, as we learnt from my mother, he had even *more* to offer. He had a brother who was a Canon of Ely (a diocese which would have scored a bull's eye with my mother, always quick to display her Cambridge connections; my mother held the clergy, particularly canons, archdeacons and rural deans, in high social esteem, my aunt Emily had once been courted by a curate, but he had been too High; my father tended to have clergymen friends, not because he was drawn to their status, but because he believed in the importance of their mission). But he also had a niece, Margiad Evans, who *wrote*, and of whom he was rightly proud. She had even had two novels published, both of them set in the Forest of Dean. This indeed is when I pricked up my ears. I was very proud of living in a town in which Thackeray had written, and of living in a house that had been lived in by Sarah Grand (though none of us had read any of her novels, my mother and I at least liked to mention the fact). I prized literary associations.

On one memorable occasion, my father and I had been travelling to London, to take in a visit to a museum and lunch at Snow's. We got into a compartment in which there was already one passenger: an old man with a long white beard and dressed, from head to foot, in black corduroy, and wearing a funny, floppy tie, of a style that would have quite defeated my mother. We sat opposite him. He was reading a book, holding it very close to his eyes, so that I could see both sides of the dust-jacket. On the back, there was the photograph of the reader opposite, there could be no doubt about it, the faces and the flowing beards matched, and there were the black corduroy and funny tie, of course in miniature, like a dwarf replica, and in black-and-white that missed the high colour of the face and the forget-me-not blue eyes. On the front was the name of the author: Aloysius (which I mentally pronounced, never having encountered a name so extraordinary, *Alloyshus*) Horn, and the title of the book, which I cannot remember. I was immensely excited by this discovery: here we were sitting opposite a man, almost in touching distance, who had written a book. What is more, he was reading the book that he had written. Indeed, so engrossed was he in it that he seemed to be quite unaware of our presence. I wanted my father to share in my amazing discovery, so I nudged him on the forearm. He looked up, rather crossly, from the *Westminster Gazette*; but when, with an expressive, and, as I hoped, discreet, movement of the head, I indicated the book held up high with the bearded face on the back, and the same bearded face, in bright colours, and multiplied by ten, behind it, I could see at once that his interest had been aroused. Unlike me, he was sitting at an oblique angle to the reader, so that, instead of having one full-face superimposed upon another full-face much magnified, he could see partly round the side of the book and get a glancing view of the face in majestic, bearded semi-profile: the sage totally absorbed in his own printed words. After knocking out his pipe and then filling it again – an operation I knew well as being designed to gain time before he decided what to do next – he cleared his throat, and, in a bold effort to separate the photograph from the living face (the blue eyes were now watering slightly), he tapped the reader on the knee, and asked, rather engagingly: 'I seem to have seen your face somewhere before,' (he had, indeed, a few seconds earlier, on the back of the dust-jacket), 'excuse my indiscretion, but are you not Aloysius Horn (he pronounced it *Alloishus* – I had to give my father credit for having picked up a thing or two, almost as if he hadn't noticed) the well-known traveller?' (this was quite a new revelation of my father's charms, for I had never known him to talk like a blurb before, and had forgotten, for the moment, that he too was, vaguely, in the publishing line). Our *vis-à-vis* did not seem in the least bit put out by this direct approach; on the contrary, he seemed almost to have expected it (perhaps he had travelled all the way from Hastings, or at least from Wadhurst, without' anyone getting into his compartment, so that the book had rested on the seat beside him, still with the back cover facing up). Smiling most affably, he acknowledged, in a very high-pitched voice, that he was indeed Aloysius Horn; 'the well-known traveller' was not actually spoken, but was implied in the slight pause that followed this self-identification.

The rest of the journey was spent most agreeably, I think for all three concerned. The traveller-author talked about his travels and his books – this was the latest one, only just out, to catch the Christmas readership and then there were a lot more to come. Then they talked about South Africa, Bechuanaland, Basutoland, Matabeleland, Swaziland, Somaliland, Egypt, and the Soudan – my father was now getting at least one country a turn ahead of the bearded author, rattling down the homeward track, roughly in the order of his own rather chaotic African career and, as he tended to equate literature with travel, and admired both Conrad and Kipling, he was obviously excited thus to meet the living combination of the two. Aloysius Horn seemed equally pleased; his journey had turned out well worthwhile, and, perhaps in the following years, he would make regular trips to and from Tunbridge Wells, in the hope of a repeat performance. All the while, I looked on in wonder; my father had grown several feet in my esteem, and I was actually seeing a real author and was listening to him talking about his work. I knew my father too was unusually pleased, for he spent the rest of the day, in London, addressing me as 'old boy' (I was II) and humming Gilbert & Sullivan tunes, always a sign that he was in exceptionally good humour.

Some weeks later Aloysius Horn turned up all at once in the house: not the moving, coloured enlargement, but the photograph on the back of his book. My mother had got it out of Boots' circulating library in the Pantiles. Over lunch my father asked her what she thought of it. 'Rather dull, and very badly written', she said. I admired my mother's literary judgment, but I did not like my only living author to be dismissed so curtly, and put it down to the fact that she had been annoyed at having missed so great an occasion. My father failed to rise, making no comment, and got up soon afterwards, saying that it was time for his afternoon walk with the dalmatians.

A few weeks after this literary encounter, Mr Evans's elderly maid brought round a note for my mother, saying that she would wait for an answer. It was an invitation for me to go to tea at No. 69 at 3.50 on the following Saturday. My mother accepted for me and I was told about the invitation when I got back from school. I was a bit surprised that he should have asked me on my own, but put it down to the fact that he probably wanted to talk to me about Shrewsbury. On the Saturday, I pulled at the enormous bell that rang from deep inside the dark mysterious house. The elderly maid opened the door, took my school cap and hung it up on a hat-stand that had already sprouted a varied crop of headgear: four caps, two panamas, a bowler, a top-hat, and a homburg. She opened the

Still Life

door into a big room at the back, facing onto a dank garden,
saying: 'Mr Evans is expecting you'. It did not look as if he
were; for, without the help of his sticks, he was engaged in
climbing, with slow deliberation, up two steel steps, thence
onto a platform lined with rubber matting, and then down the
other side, coming full-round in a semi-circle, and starting all
over again: up, one, two, pause, down, one, two. 'Don't mind
me,' he said, on reaching the top platform the second time, 'it's
my exercises; sit down over there and make yourself
comfortable, I have six more to do, it won't take long'. Though
I had never seen an instrument quite like the steps, I was used
to invalids, having had tea with many, and I realised that this
was not some sort of peculiar game and that he was not doing it
for fun, like my *Ben Hur* chariot races on chairs. I felt flattered
that he should have gone on with the slow, deliberate
movements in my presence. It made me feel at home in the big
house with the heavy velvet curtains. It was as if he had let me
into one of his secrets. And, when he had completed six more
ups and downs, he turned to me, and said: 'That's it for today',
with a sad, slow smile, and made his way to an embroidered
bell-pull. The maid came almost at once, folded up the steps,
putting them away in a corner. 'Did Mr Evans do his dozen?'
she asked me, smiling. I felt even more at home. 'Time for tea,'
said my host, leading the way through the hall to the
dining-room. Tea certainly looked a major operation, one far
more elaborate than the exercises on the collapsible steel and
rubber steps. I had been out to tea many times in the big houses
in Nevill Park, but I had never seen an array as magnificent as
the one that confronted me on Mr Evans's enormous dining-
room table: a thick, glistening, stiff white table-cloth on which
two places were laid, Mr Evans's at the head of the table, and
mine on his right, facing the dark, wintry garden. By each,
there were two lots of big cups in flower patterns, three silver
knives and three silver forks. In front of Mr Evans's place stood,
like ungainly storks, a pair of huge silver teapots, with little

silver taps, as well as long, graceful spouts, each on a tall stand, and under which burnt a bluish flame. The rest of the table was strewn with tiered edifices like miniature pagodas, also in silver, and supporting, from a series of branches, plates of thinly-cut sandwiches, muffins, crumpets, scones, a chocolate cake, a cherry cake, a seed cake, an iced cake, and a yellow cake with a cream and jam filling. 'China or Indian?' asked Mr Evans, and, on my opting for the former, he turned down the flame under the left-hand silver machine, and brought out from his waistcoat pocket a gold whole-hunter on a chain, unhooking it and placing it opened up, beside his place. '3½ minutes we'll give it, I think, don't you?' as if I were the best judge. Then having rung the maid from a bell under the table, he sat in silence, listening to the ticking of the gold watch, while the maid came and removed the other silver stork, after extinguishing its flame. It was a magnificent tea, though Mr Evans confined himself to very thinly-cut slices of buttered toast, explaining that he had to be careful about what he ate, or, he smiled with an air of complicity, he would get into trouble with his doctor and with Mrs Elliott; but, he added, there was all the time in the world – the watch had gone back onto its chain and into his pocket – and I must try everything, but that Mrs Elliott was especially good at scones and cakes: 'she's Scotch, you know,' he added, as though in explanation. He watched me with benevolent interest as I worked my way from pagoda to pagoda and from tier to tier. The blue flame was relit twice, after more water had been called for and the watch brought out.

Mr Evans talked quite a lot about his niece Margiad Evans, and I told him about our encounter with Aloysius Horn; out came his slow smile at this, 'he's a bit of a fraud, you know, well, let us say, he exaggerates'. This should have been a blow, as it appeared to reduce the importance of our encounter, but I felt that I must defer to my host's judgment, especially as he was the uncle of a well-known novelist, one of whose books was upstairs in Boot's in the Pantiles. He promised that the next time his clever niece came to stay with him, he'd let me know, as he was sure that she and I would find a lot to talk about together. By this euphoric stage I was eating downwards from the sixth pagoda. There had been no reference to Shrewsbury, nor would there be at any of my subsequent visits. I certainly had not been invited so as to hear his views about the school. Once I had reached the bottom of the sixth pagoda, he asked me if I had had enough; I said – and no doubt looked – that I had indeed. 'Shall we move then?' he suggested, getting to his feet, and shuffling off ahead of me, with his usual slow purposefulness. Because every movement cost him a considerable effort and must have caused him quite a lot of pain, everything he did – even taking out his watch – seemed to acquire a special importance, as if each gesture had been part of some mysterious ceremonial and as if the act of opening a door announced the revelation of a close-kept secret. Indeed, when we reached the hall, instead of returning to the drawing-room, he made his way to a green-baize door at the far end. 'Now', he said, turning the white knob, 'let's get down to serious business.'

I followed him into a long room with French windows at the far end, the curtains undrawn, the radiators giving out a gentle, even heat. He turned on the ceiling lights, revealing a magnificent pinkish rug, and a small S-shaped chair in white and gilt, facing both ways, as the only article of furniture. Along both walls were some thirty picture-frames, each covered by a small green curtain on runners and surmounted by a long brass light. He started at the near end, turning on the little light and pulling aside the curtain: a tiny water-colour of a field of ripe corn in movement under a huge, luminous, windy sky with stretched out streaky clouds: 'David Cox', he said, 'what do you think of *that?*' What I thought of it was that it was stunningly beautiful, in quite a different class from any of the many water-colours, including those, highly accomplished, painted by my mother, that I had seen in scores of Tunbridge Wells drawing-rooms. He turned out the little light, and the cornfield and the bright sky disappeared modestly behind the little green curtain. 'This is Norfolk, too', he said, moving to the next picture, another Cox: dark pines against a foreground of sand, coiling grass and red poppies. And so we moved slowly down the near side of the room, Mr Evans leaning on only one stick so as to leave his hand free to draw back the enticing curtains: Old Crome, a darkening landscape, the interior of a railway station under a glass roof, with rays of sunshine, an old-fashioned green engine with an enormous stack, and carriages like coaches; a leafy summer scene, a yellow country road between tall hedgerows, a white lighthouse and an inlet of white-flecked grey water, a brownish-yellow beach shelving steeply and with rotting black hulks and a red dinghy upside-down; a grey cathedral outlined against a mobile, yet placid sky at dusk; the tall grey flint tower, with lozenges of black and white, of a country church surrounded by clumps of elms and a very dark green yew; a humped wooden bridge over a still stream, or possibly just a drainage ditch, between two fields of tall grasses and purple weeds. Everywhere, the amazing sky in movement, muted, peaceful, not threatening, in restrained and opaque shades, never strident or blinding, the East Anglian sky, and a wonderful range of gentle greens, washed-out blues, and pale pinks, reds, and beiges. They were all landscapes, nearly all of them diminutive, delicate, modest, and perfect miniatures dating from the seventeen-nineties to the eighteen-thirties. We took three-quarters of an hour to get round the room, Mr Evans sitting down, every now and then, on the white and gilt chair, while I returned to this or that green curtain, pulling it aside, for a second look. 'The Norfolk School', he said, 'though some of them are set in Suffolk' (I think, too, there was one russet-sailed Colne or Orwell barge in an estuary, for the colour seemed familiar). He added, with his kind, slow-spreading smile, that it was an unusual collection of very early English water-colours and that he had inherited it from his mother, a descendant of David Cox. He hoped I had enjoyed seeing it, especially as it was from my part of England, adding that there was more to come, two more rooms, in fact, of later Norfolk works. But that would be for another time. Now it was time that I was going, as he had told my mother that I would be back by 6.30. I shook hands with my host and Mrs Elliott appeared in the hall and handed me my cap. I walked up the road, very happy and excited, and, when I got home, I told my mother about the wonderful water-colours. As she had been a pupil of Barlow-Wood, a well-known late Victorian Ipswich painter, she was very interested to hear about the Norfolk School water-colours. But she never saw any of them, indeed never got inside no. 69. I returned there many times for tea and further viewings, meeting, on one of these Saturday visits, the novelist niece. She told me a lot about Mr Evans; he had never married, had always lived alone, though Mrs Elliott had been in his service for thirty years. She spoke of her uncle with a mixture of affection and amusement: the fussy little green curtains amused her most, but I pointed out that they were very necessary, as water-colours were very delicate and could easily fade if exposed to strong light.

Then the invitations grew less regular, and finally stopped altogether, while Mr Evans was no longer seen, struggling along on his two sticks, towards the Grove. One day I saw the blinds were down; shortly after that I met Mrs Elliott, dressed in black. Mr Evans had died at home. He had had his bed moved into the drawing-room, as he had found it more and more difficult to get upstairs. She told me that the pictures were going to the Canon's at Ely. For many years, I missed the slow-spreading smile, the deliberate movements, the quiet, unaffected kindness and discreet attentiveness, the wonderful teas and the beautiful, little pictures.

Some years later, I visited Margiad Evans, Mrs Peggy Williams – she was married to a naval officer and he was away serving on convoys – at her white cottage in Llangarron, near Ross-on-Wye. She had me put up in the village. I sent her some of my short stories, one of which, about a Polish airman who had come down in the Somme and had been taken in by a French farmer, had been published in *Life & Letters Today*. She sent me a nice letter back, with the stories, which she said she had read with interest. Even so, she added, she thought that after the War, I should go back to history. It was no doubt sound advice; anyhow, I followed it, went back to history, though it became history of an increasingly peculiar sort. I could not paint, but I could still be a miniaturist. A little later, Margiad Evans sent me her latest book, a sad, bleak little autobiography about watching the changing seasons from the windows of her white cottage. With the book came a letter in which she told me that her husband was back from the Navy. After the War, I lost touch with her completely; and it was only recently, on reading Moira Dearnley's biography, that I learnt that she had been forced by persistent ill-health to leave Llangarron, and that she had died, in March 1958, in the Kent & Sussex hospital, Tunbridge Wells. She had represented my second encounter with a living author. No. 69 was sold. I do not know who moved into it. Last time I went past it, I noticed that it had been painted a pale cream, with the windowsills and surrounds and the columns of the huge porch picked out in light chocolate. There was a vase of flowers in white trellis-work, hanging above the entrance. Mr Evans would not have liked that. I did not feel any regrets; I had been inside the house when it had contained old Mr Evans, the smiling and efficient Mrs Elliott, and the wonderful little water-colours so few people had ever seen.

EPILOGUE

For one so slight, thin, and apparently fragile, my mother had all at once begun to display an unexpected reserve of physical strength. While still in the Clarence Nursing Home – for the last time, as it turned out – she managed to throw her night-table right across the room at the night-nurse. Matron received a chair in full flight, the other nurses, various missiles of furniture. The night-nurse, Matron and the personnel of the Clarence were all in the plot to poison her; they had been put up to it by my sister and myself, the originators of the plot with my aunt Mabel, once my mother's favourite sister. So she would not see my sister and me; and we could only communicate with her through my friend Richard Spilsbury – the surname had done the trick – to whom she entrusted her wedding-ring, her engagement ring, her pocket watch, and her jewellery, so that they would not fall into our hands or those of Mabel. Richard managed to persuade her that the best course of action would be to take the black saloon he had laid on – it had in fact been provided by the Clarence – and travel in it with him to Northampton, where she would be safe from all the conspirators; they would be able to effect their escape from Tunbridge Wells before any of us found out. So my mother ended up in the chintzed drawing-room of St Andrew's Hospital, Northampton. When my sister or I went to see her there, sometimes she would recognise us and would talk quite sensibly, and sometimes she would not know who we were. Once, she told me, in confidence, that my sister was dying of tuberculosis, adding that I must keep it a secret, as my brother-in-law did not know. Her sister Mabel remained a consistent demon figure, both on her good and her bad days.

My mother, who was quite a forceful personality, despite her slight appearance, had managed to establish herself in a very comfortable cretonned armchair by one of the French windows, facing onto the extensive gardens, the rhododendrons, and the herbaceous borders. It was the best seat in the room, but the borders were too well-kept, the flowers were marshalled in serried ranks by colours, reds here, blues there, pinks there. The garden was too vast; it had an institutional look, it seemed to be masquerading as an ordinary private garden, such as one might glimpse from a drawing-room in Broadwater Down; and this is just what it was doing, for it was indeed an institutional garden in the grounds of a private mental hospital; and the French windows, like all the doors to the chintzed drawing-room, were double-locked. My mother could not walk through the French windows to take a closer look at the borders or sit on one of the white seats in the sunshine, unless she were accompanied. Much of the day, she sat in her armchair, with her back to the other ladies, knitting, or looking at the garden. Some of the other ladies seemed much worse than my mother. One kept on making whoops; another ceaselessly opened and shut her mouth, emitting a gobbling noise, several talked to themselves incessantly, one howled like a dog. My mother said to me, for once looking round: 'They are all *nice* people, you know, you can see that'. I could see that; they all wore sensible clothes and woollen cardigans and had good accents and were elaborately polite; several talked nonsense in lady-like tones. My mother seemed to have established quite friendly relations with two or three of them; one was a vicar's widow, another was a doctor's daughter, and there was the almost inevitable Cambridge graduate – 'but not from Girton, a pity'. Touching her forehead with her long, thin hand, and lowering her voice to what she may have imagined to have been a whisper, but which was perfectly distinct, as always, and carried right across the big room, she commented, for my benefit: 'They are all MAD, you know.' On the same occasion – one of her good days – when a gentle Jamaican nurse came with the tea, she observed, in a tone meant only to be heard by myself, but which crossed the chintzed room: 'She's very good, very willing, but, of course, she is a native, BLACK, you know.' The Jamaican nurse seemed to be quite used to such comments. Occasionally, she would ask me what I had been doing, but her attention would soon wander when I started to tell her. More often, she enquired about Mrs Martin, wondering if she were looking after the house. Once or twice, in moments of mercifully rare lucidity, she said it was awful to be cooped up in this way and that she wished she could get back to 5a, the house must be in a dreadful mess; so was her hair, it was time she had it done by the nice lady on Grove Hill, Elaine. But, more often, she wandered on about plots. 'It had all been Mabel's doing, I was a fool, I should have foreseen it.' The place was an awful parody of a middle-class drawing-room, the flowers were arranged too artfully, and the nurses were carrying large keys on wooden numbered handles everywhere they went.

So the house remained empty, save when I was there for brief periods. I got Mrs Martin to come every day, as before, and she agreed. It was a rather desperate bid for continuity on the part of both of us. The house seemed to be waiting, leaderless, like a troop waiting for an inspection that never came. Here was every object in place, according to an order that had been worked out by my mother. The little red. account-book was in its niche at the top of her desk, the sealing-wax was in its allotted place. I did what I could for the geraniums, they seemed to grow on their own, as if, unlike the other objects, they were unaware of my mother's absence. Mrs Martin polished, dusted and hoovered, opened and shut windows; and, at 11, she made herself coffee, very weak, with milk, sitting in the kitchen, with the dining-room door held open. Every now and then, she remade my mother's bed and put hot water-bottles in it. She went on coming, from 9 till 12 every week-day, for the next four years. On Grove Hill, in Claremont Road, on Mount Sion, in the High Street, in Chapel Place and in the Pantiles, my mother's friends would stop me and ask me how she was. 'Much the same', was the answer, because she did not seem to get any worse, and survived several bouts of pneumonia. Of course, I knew that she was not going to get any better and that she would not be coming back. But I kept on Mrs Martin. I was not going to cut the last link.

When my mother died – quite suddenly – at 85 – I was in Leeds. We had the funeral in King Charles. There was hardly

anyone there, because we had put her death ('daughter of Dr
J.A. Swindale, MD', for I knew she would have wanted that)
only in *The Times,* and most of her friends read the *Telegraph.*
So it was a very quiet funeral; most of her friends did not even
know that she had come back to Tunbridge Wells. My sister
had all the contents of her bedroom, including the big leather
hat-box; I had all the rest. Going through her desk, I found all
my school reports, cuttings about my prizes and Postmaster-
ship, all the picture postcards I had sent her from France, old
copies of the *Kent & Sussex Courier* relating to my sister's
successes at tennis, eighty uncut packs of playing cards,
thirty-five unused scoring pads with sharpened gold pencils. I
went through her sketching pads, wondering why she had given
up water-colours once she had got married. Some of the
sketches were unfinished. My sister had all the clothes; I don't
know what she did with them. I did not want to keep the house
any more and, after a year, I closed it up, taking everything
away. In fact, I took away more than I had thought. I can still
situate, after twenty years, each object in its assigned place in
my mother's irreversible order, in the drawing room and in her
bedroom. I went to Mrs Martin's funeral at the Battery. Kate
could still just be alive; she would be about my mother's age if
she were. All my mother's friends are dead. I can still hear her
distinct, rather emphatic, very self-assured speech: 'Richard,
you look a *shack*' (perhaps a reference to the way of life of the
local hermits) and see her erect figure, in a grey cardigan, her
face in profile silhouetting her sharp nose, as she sits, over tea,
by the French windows opening onto the balcony, with the
sound of the bowls coming through from the Grove Bowling
Club.

Printed in Great Britain
by Amazon